WHEELS OF THUNDER

P. J. Richardson &
Robert Darden

THOMAS NELSON PUBLISHERS
Nashville • Atlanta • London • Vancouver

Published in Nashville, Tennessee, by Thomas Nelson, Inc., and distributed in Canada by Word Communications, Ltd., Richmond, British Columbia, and in the United Kingdom by Word (UK), Ltd., Milton Keynes, England.

Scripture quotations are from the NEW KING JAMES VERSION of the Bible. Copyright © 1979, 1980, 1982, 1990, 1994 Thomas Nelson, Inc., Publishers.

Library of Congress Cataloging-in-Publication Data
Richardson, P. J.
  Wheels of thunder / by P. J. Richardson and Robert Darden.
    p.   cm.
  ISBN 0-7852-7223-2 (pbk.)
  1. Automobile racing drivers—Biography. 2. Christian biography.
3. Christian life. I. Darden, Bob, 1954– . II. Title.
GV1032.A1R53 1997
796.7´2´0922—dc21
[B]
                                        96–37194
                                           CIP

Printed in the United States of America

1 2 3 4 5 6 7 QBP 03 02 01 99 98 97

Dedicated to my grandparents:
Robert Fulton Darden,
Esther Perkins Chatelain,
Stephen Brunson Owens,
Margaret Allie Owens

—Robert Darden

Dedicated to my best friend and wife of
twenty-six years, Billie

—P. J. Richardson

CONTENTS

Acknowledgments

P. J. Richardson and Robert Darden would like to thank:

- **Max Helton, Ann Conway, and Ron Pegram**
  Motor Racing Outreach
  Smith Tower, Suite 405
  Highway 29 North
  Harrisburg, PA 28075

- **Hunter Floyd**
  Motorsports Ministries
  3867 Bennett Drive
  Indianapolis, IN 46254

- **Bob Dyar**
  Carolina Sports Outreach, Inc.
  9432 Sardis Glen Drive
  Matthews, NC 28105

- **Penzoil**

- **Jasper Motorsports**

DARRELL WALTRIP

Driver/Owner
#17
Western Auto Parts America
Darrell Waltrip Chevrolet Monte Carlo

When Darrell Waltrip came along, things changed. Darrell is the link between Richard Petty and Jeff Gordon. He helped elevate the sport from regional to international, from family to corporate. He went from dominating the short tracks of the Midwest to becoming a major force in NASCAR, winning the Winston Cup three times (1981, 1982, and 1985). His career victory total of eighty-four leads all active drivers by a comfortable margin.

It would be a serious mistake, however, to dismiss Darrell Waltrip as a legend or an icon. He's still a passionate competitor, a motor-racing innovator, and a threat to win every time he guns his distinctive white/red/blue/black Parts America Monte Carlo down every straightaway from Watkins Glen to Phoenix.

Like most kids in the fifties and sixties, I grew up in a Christian family. My dad was a church deacon in Owensboro, Kentucky. I was a typical kid—I went to all of the vacation Bible schools, training unions, choirs, Sunday schools, church every Sunday, prayer meeting every Wednesday night, and visitation on Thursday night! I did that for most of my childhood.

My grandmother Waltrip was probably the person most

responsible for my being so involved in the church. She lived alone near our church and I spent a lot of time with her. When you're older, as she was, well, church is like home. If the doors were open, she was going to be there! I stayed with her a lot to keep her company—and so away I went to church!

I think I was about twelve when I made a public profession of faith. I remember being in front of the church and professing my faith, and then getting dunked. It was a Sunday and I can still remember going up and getting in that big ol' tank. I was pretty nervous about it. But I got baptized.

I was baptized three times, as a matter of fact. The first time, when I was twelve. A few years later, we moved from one part of Owensboro to another part and changed churches around the same time. When I was about sixteen, I got baptized again, but I can't even tell you how or why that happened. It was something that particular church did to show renewal of faith, which I guess I needed—even though I was only sixteen years old.

It happened a third time when this particular tent revival came to town. (We had a lot of those in that part of the country.) They were going to baptize people in the Ohio. Well, I thought this sounded pretty cool. Getting washed in the river sounded like a good idea to me—it was unusual to me, and it *might* have some special effect that I wasn't aware of! So I went down on a Sunday evening and got baptized in the Ohio River.

Like all teenagers who spent a lot of time in the church, I think once I was able to make the choice of whether I *wanted* to go to church or not, I quit going. You go through that period of time where—and I think probably most young people do it—all of a sudden, you're old enough to make decisions for yourself and you're not going to church Sunday and you're not going to church Wednesday. So that's just the end of that. You go through a number of years just like that.

And that's where I was. I got busy racing, making a living, and I got married. The last thing I had time for was to go to church. I didn't go to church until 1981, when I started going regularly again.

My wife, Stevie, was the reason I went back. She's a strong Christian lady. She grew up in the church and it was very, very important to her. She thought it was very important to our relationship and our marriage as well.

Also, we had some friends who were going to a church meeting on Wednesday nights in Nashville. The church met in Hillsboro High School and Dr. Cortez Cooper was the minister. This was a breakaway church from the big First Presbyterian Church of Nashville. Dr. Cooper didn't agree with some of First Church's theology, so he started a new church. They had services on Sunday in the auditorium.

I'd always used the excuse, "Well, I'm out of town; I can't do that. I'm racing on Sundays." So now all of a sudden, we've got a Wednesday night option. So our friends said, "You need to go down here with us on Wednesday nights." Since I'm always at home on Wednesday nights, I finally said, "Oh, all right, if that's what I've got to do, I'll do it."

They'd have a covered dish supper and then they'd have services. So I went. Man! The first couple of Wednesday nights in the high school cafeteria with no air conditioning were hotter 'n hades! But Dr. Cooper turned out to be a super, super guy. He was a great teacher. I got to know him pretty well, and soon I really liked him. He knew about my profession. It wasn't long before we really struck up a good relationship.

And by virtue of Wednesday night services, meeting Dr. Cooper, and kind of getting back in the swing of things, I recommitted myself to the Lord in July of 1983 in that cafeteria. And I have been going strong ever since! (I didn't even have to get baptized again. We all felt like I'd had my share!)

Memorable Moment

Certainly, the first race I ever won, which was in 1975 at Nashville, Tennessee—my home track. That was big.

Then the next memorable time was in 1987, the Sunday after we'd had Jessica on Wednesday. Nineteen-eighty-seven wasn't a particularly good year for me. I'd started a new team with the Tide car and we hadn't had the success we thought we should have. We had no wins. Jessica was born on September 17. The next race was Martinsville. I showed up for the race, and Sunday morning there was a little rosebud in the seat of my race car with a note that said, "Win one for me, Daddy!"

Of course, this was the first time I'd ever been called "Daddy." I won that race that day! That made it incredibly special.

In 1992, when Sarah was born midweek, and at the very next race I went to, in Bristol, Tennessee, there was no rosebud, no note this time. But I won that race as well!

Those are pretty special.

Then, of course, the 1989 Daytona 500, which is NASCAR's Super Bowl, that was special as well.

But when you think about it, every time you get to race is special. A racer can go back and talk about any race he won; it might have been in 1977 and he'll go, "Yeah, it was me and Cale, we were coming down the back straightaway at Michigan and he booted me a little bit and I booted him back and I beat him to the line by a car length. He was driving the old #27 and I was driving #11. I led by eighty-two laps that day. . . ." They remember with *that* kind of detail.

RANDY TOLSMA

Driver
#61
Xpress Motorsports
IWX Trucking
Chevy Truck

It's hard to picture Randy Tolsma doing anything but racing . . . except, maybe, painting pictures. Randy is a popular artist specializing in photo-realistic airbrush paintings of racing–related subjects!

He's also one heck of a racer, with a room full of trophies in the Midget, Super Modified Outlaws, Super Midget Outlaws, USAC Silver Crown, and Clark Midgets. He comes by it honestly—his father, Ron, raced Super Modifieds on the West Coast CAMRA circuit for decades.

Nothing could compare with 1996 for Randy. It started with his first-ever start at the Indianapolis 500, thirty-first in the McCormack Motorsports 1993 Lola. It ended when Randy was offered a regular ride with the powerful Xpress Motorsports team on the fast-growing NASCAR Supertruck Series in the red, white, and yellow #61 Chevy truck.

It's the kind of year Randy would like to paint a picture of and frame forever!

My testimony is a little different because both my wife and I came to know the Lord about the same time, but from completely different circumstances. Neither of us grew up in a Christian home. My family believed that there was a God—we just didn't know anything about Him. Both of my parents were saved as children, but there was no discipleship from there on, so they didn't learn anything. We really didn't attend church.

As I got older, my go-cart races were always on Sunday. In school, I was embarrassed when anyone brought up Jesus or the Bible because I didn't know anything about *either* subject. And I'm one who doesn't like to be on the outside.

Still, it was a happy childhood; I had a functional, loving family. Everything was on track by the time I was a teenager. My racing career was going well and I won a lot; I was a star athlete from Little League baseball to high school football.

I truly believed that there *was* a God, but I didn't know anything about Him. I had a yearning. I knew that there was a purpose for all of us on this earth, and that there had to be more out there than just racing. I wanted to know more. My biggest drawback was always that I didn't know anything about church, so I was uncomfortable going.

I began to work at a shop where the boss and his daughter worked alongside me, and I soon discovered that they were both Christians. Gary Hall and Jennifer Boyd witnessed very subtly to me. They planted the seed. We'd talk a little bit. At one point, they even laughed when I told them that I thought I would go to heaven because I was a good person. As kindly as they knew how, they told me that there is more to it than that. They were caring, loving people.

Gary went to a real structured church, while Jennifer was going to a Baptist church that was just starting out and meeting in a day-care center. I thought that kind of setting wouldn't be quite as scary to go into. It was casual, it wasn't formal—it was something I could handle. Jennifer invited me and my wife, Tiffanie, and we went.

Baptists, of course, always have quite a salvation message. It gave me questions. The next Saturday the pastor and his wife came over to our house. We talked and asked questions for quite a while. And when Tiffanie and I were both ready, we accepted the Lord that day.

Has it been difficult to maintain your faith in the nomadic life of motor racing?

When we lived in Boise, racing was my weekend job—I needed a regular job to support it. When we moved back to Indianapolis, it became our life. Tiffanie worked at the Indianapolis Raceway Park (and still does), and I raced full-time.

We'd race late on Saturday night, get done at 1 A.M., and wander over to a little club in town. It would then be hard to get up and go to church. We were slow finding a church in Indianapolis. We visited several but didn't find what we wanted. As a result, we struggled in our faith. We soon got caught up in the racing life, which is what I'd wanted to do for twenty years. We got away from our prayers and we fell down a little.

But the Lord woke us up pretty hard with reality—and that put us back on track in a hurry! In Indianapolis, we'd raced for two national championships in the Midget and the Silver Crown divisions. But the team quit running the Midgets halfway through the season; then I was abruptly fired from the Silver Crowns for no reason at all. Or maybe there was a reason. With the people we hung around, I think we got tied up in the rumor mill. Rumors got started. And they just took off until they got back to the owner. He heard that I wasn't happy and was looking for another ride, so he fired me.

So, suddenly, we got this wake-up call. Believe me, it got us both serious in a hurry. We got back into our Christian walk, probably stronger than ever. Our lives had changed from the security of Boise, and now we were facing hard times.

It was funny how we found our church in Indianapolis. There was one church that we did *not* want to go to, just because they were real forceful in their pamphlets and sent a lot in the mail. I always figured that if they had that much energy, they weren't going to be comfortable with me only being able to show up one Sunday out of four because of my race schedule. I told Tiffanie, "I just don't want to visit there."

But we had some friends who said, "We know *exactly* where we want to take you—this is the perfect church for you two." It was Bethesda Baptist Church, the one I didn't want to go to! Still, we went and discovered that they had a fabulous pastor and music program, great programs for kids—it's a large church, but they knew your name after the first week. We just felt at home and knew that was the place to be. Our pastor, Donald Tyler, is also the chaplain for the Indianapolis Indians minor league baseball team. He understands a pro athlete's situation.

We've also gotten involved with the pastors on the racing circuit, particularly Hunter Floyd and Ronald Askew, who travels the Midget, Sprint Car, and Silver Crown circuits. I've had some great counseling from Sam and Ann Conway, Max Helton, Ron Pegram, and I've been asked to speak at the chapel service for the Busch Grand National Series for Ron. They're all fabulous people. They'll go places no one else can or will go.

We have a house Bible study every Tuesday for anyone who might want to seek the Lord or know what the Bible says. If anyone is going through a problem, there's someone who will listen. It's not a structured Bible study where you have to be there every week.

Memorable Moment

There are a few. Certainly one of the big ones for us was June 19, 1993, my second race in Indianapolis. We were from Idaho, completely unknown. It was the first night of the Past Masters Series, which brought the retired drivers back to Raceway Park for an exhibition-type race. There was a Midget race that night. We showed up out of nowhere and won! It was on national TV, and the announcers couldn't pronounce my name—that's how unknown we were. We beat the best of the best. That was good for our career, as well as exciting.

The second was the month of May in 1996 at the Indianapolis Speedway. It was the first year I tried to make the Indianapolis 500. The Speedway itself was incredible; the experience was incredible. To think that I was finally there and got that chance to drive at over two hundred miles per hour at Indy was amazing.

As for the race going as I thought it should—well, it didn't. I'd wanted the whole month to be smooth and go well, but it probably went as bad as it could have except that I wasn't hurt! My car didn't arrive until the last weekend and there was a big struggle to get up to speed in a hurry and make dramatic changes to a race car that you don't make quickly. I really didn't think I'd be able to handle it.

But our church was praying for us each and every day. That was the first time in my life I'd ever felt being lifted up in prayer, and it went on throughout that month. Even though nothing was going according to plan, this was what I'd hoped for for years, and sometimes you only get one opportunity to race at Indy. I felt a peace about it.

We ended up crashing on the last day. I was able to walk out of that hospital knowing that it was all for a reason and that I would be taken care of. That's probably the first time in my life that I really felt that power of prayer.

It was exciting to know that God's hand was in it. And it was exciting to know that I'm still one of the few people in this world who have had that opportunity.

The thing about this sport is, while you hate the tragedies, they give you excellent opportunities to witness. We were lucky enough to have a local TV commentator who knew that I was a believer, and they interviewed me after Scott Braden's death. He said, "As a racer, how do you deal with this?" Then he asked, "As a man of faith, how do you deal with this?" What an opportunity! I had a little spot there on the news and it was live! I was real thankful to God for that opportunity, that I was prepared, and that the Holy Spirit had the words for me to speak. Hopefully some people heard those words.

My career hasn't been easy—not very many are. I've come to realize that people are watching my attitude as things go badly. Others may use their trips to Victory Lane as their witness and are blessed that way. That's been a real revelation lately, that God can use winning, losing, crashing, whatever. And I praise God for that.

DENNIS SWAN

Chief Steward
Championship Auto Racing Teams

Dennis Swan joined Indy Car in 1995 as vice president of logistics in preparation for assuming the pivotal job of chief steward in 1996. He spent the year studying under the current steward, the legendary Wally Dallenbach, Sr., veteran of 180 Indy Car races and chief steward for more than a decade.

Dennis Swan's new job description includes overseeing Indy Car officials at the racetrack and overall responsibilities for the safe and competitive conduct of each Indy Car event.

Despite whatever natural trepidations he might have had initially, Dennis shoulders the important position with the full confidence and support of virtually everyone associated with Indy Car racing.

I came from a Christian family, but not one where you learned about the Lord. I came from a family that said, "People are basically God-fearing and so you go to church." So I went to church periodically, certainly not on a regular basis, when I was younger. Then when I was in junior high school I stopped attending until later in my life.

I started working on race cars when I was sixteen in 1964. That was my entire life. When I turned eighteen, I went down for the draft. I was going to end up getting drafted into the Marine

Corps, so I joined the navy reserves. I was still racing at that time, working on race cars. I ended up overseas in 1968.

I came home and started racing again. Eventually, I was involved in a Can-Am Series for a company in Connecticut, Young American Racing. When that job ended, which racing jobs usually do, I moved out to the West Coast and started working for Roy Woods Racing and the Formula 5000 Series in '73. I also married that year.

When you're doing your travel thing, you're gone forever. In '74 and '75 I lived in Canada and I worked for Formula Racing. I worked at Parnelli's for a couple of years. Then I went to work at Chaparral Cars and we went to Indy. I was involved with the winning car twice at Indianapolis, and we won some national championships.

Then I left Chaparral Cars and went up to Michigan and started a team from the ground up for a gentleman named Doug Shierson.

I was becoming very successful. But I wasn't faithful to my wife. You have lots of opportunities on the road. I had no moral values, per se, other than the ones I invented for myself. I justified it. I wouldn't say that my marriage was falling apart, but I certainly wasn't being a proper partner.

I was running with a pretty wild, very wealthy crowd. When you run with that crowd, you forget what life's really about. You start, or attempt, to live that lifestyle. You can't because you just aren't able financially. No matter how good you do, you're never in the league that those people are in. Most of them are born in it.

From the outside, you look as if you're really having a good time and you pretty much convince yourself that you are. That's the beginning of the end, or the end of the end.

About that time, I met a lady named Julie in this town where I was living at the time, Adrian, Michigan. I don't know what happened, but I made everything work in that direction and went through a divorce. My first wife and I had no children, but it still was a difficult time. I had lost my father when I was very young, and divorce felt that traumatic, like a death in the family. So even though I orchestrated it and that's the direction that I wanted to go, it was still traumatic.

As I was going through this, I had a couple of friends named

Shawn and Gerald Davis. Gerald and I had worked together at Chaparral Cars. And Gerald was a wild man like I was. By then I'd gone on to Shierson Racing, which was the Domino's Pizza car. One day I was talking with Shawn in Indianapolis. Shawn was always a believer and really worked hard to try and help other people. As we were sitting and talking, she made the comment that no matter how successful you are, without the Lord, there's always a hole.

I had heard this before, but it had never really sunk in. All of a sudden this thing began to really nag at me. I'm sure it was the Holy Spirit working in my life. I realized that no matter where I was, there was always this emptiness and loneliness in my life. Still, I was still orchestrating the divorce and fulfilling my desires.

I went through with the marriage on August 8, 1988. Al Unser, Jr., was the best man and his wife, Shelly, stood up for Julie. I'm the godfather of Al's middle girl, Cody. So we got married and had the standard sort of ridiculous party afterward. There were about five of us in all. Then Al left for Pocono and I said, "Well, I'll see you there." That was on a Monday and I was going to take Tuesday off.

The next morning, I got a phone call from my boss, Doug, and he said, "I need to see you."

I said, "Well, you know, I was taking today off, I told you that."

Doug said, "I need to see you now."

So I went in. He was sitting in the office with his dark glasses on—remember, I'd worked for the man for seven years—and he basically said that I no longer had a job. The day after I got married!

It was a shock and I was very bitter. In retrospect, I realize now that it was one of those deals where the Lord had already started to intervene in my life. He probably intervenes all along and we just don't recognize it. I certainly didn't recognize it at that moment!

Here I had gone through a divorce and given everything away, so this was a start-over job. I'd just bought a house and there I was without a job, with a wife and her small son, which I wasn't really prepared for, either!

Fortunately, I'd made many friends and someone gave me an

opportunity to work for him in a machine shop just to fill a void. Part of the deal when I left Doug's place was that he paid me for the rest of the year too.

At this time, Julie and I were both looking for a Higher Being. We both realized that we needed something. We watched Robert Schuller on TV periodically. Actually, I'd been giving money to that ministry for three years, thinking that I needed to be doing *something*. I just felt that it was the right thing to do; I don't really know why.

I ended up getting a job for a company called True Sports in November of 1988. Steve Horn was the team manager. When the owner died, Steve was given part of the company. My title was test team manager.

So we picked up our stuff from Michigan and moved down to Indianapolis. When we first got there, we decided that we needed to find a church, so we started looking. We were still watching the Schuller program when it fit into my schedule.

I was gone a lot over the winter because when the test program started, I went out on the West Coast. I was gone two and three weeks at a time, and then I'd come back for four days, and then be gone for another couple of weeks.

While I was gone, an Evangelism Explosion group came by to see Julie. They walked up to her and asked her the same questions they ask everyone. But she had answers for them. As for me, I had no idea *what* Julie believed. We had never shared that with one another.

I came back the next day and as Julie and I were getting ready to go on a walk, this gentleman pulled up in the driveway. He got out of the car and introduced himself—Pastor Dan Summers. He was the follow-up guy for E.E. He said, "May I spend a few minutes with you?"

I said, "Sure."

So we went upstairs and sat down, and I asked a bunch of questions that had always been nagging me. Like, "How could God have built the earth in seven days when we know for a fact that it's been around for a long time?"

Pastor Summers looked at me and said, "Well, what is a day?"

Then it dawned on me. We always try and put things into something that we can grasp because we're human beings. But we're not talking about a human being. We're talking about a supernatural Being. God is supernatural. It's called faith.

We ended up talking for about two and a half hours.

When he left, we made up our minds that on Sunday we would go to Dan's church, Lincoln Baptist, which was just a mile from our house. We went and listened to Dan preach, and they had a fantastic music group, and we just got involved. In short order, we got very active. Over a couple of years, I even became one of the stewards.

Julie accepted Jesus Christ, and I became more involved and more interested and realized that this was what I needed to do. When I got involved in E.E., I finally realized what this inner peace was. It was accepting Jesus Christ as my Savior and realizing that all these sins that I committed were gone. And I did.

During this time at True Sports, we were actively pursuing one of the dreams that I'd always had, which was to build an all-American car. I was involved in that program, and I was still running the test team. We had a young driver named Scott Pruett.

So life was just going on. We were at a test in West Palm Beach with Scott, and we were getting ready for the 1990 season, in January or February, when we had a bad accident. Scott lost the brakes on the back side of the racetrack in one of the fastest sections and went off. When I got to the car, he had his helmet off, but he was pinned in the car and in a lot of pain. There were some rescue people there, but you have to orchestrate what happens. Steve, the owner, was there and we all were trying to get Scott out of the car. It quickly became obvious that there were several of us working at different means to make this happen.

At that moment, I said a prayer silently and the Lord answered me. He told me to take charge and that Scott was going to be okay. I don't know how to put it, but this inner peace set in me and I just took charge.

That's basically when I realized that God is there and He's with us all the time. And He's there to help us. That just really reaffirmed everything that was going on in my life. It also gave me the opportunity to talk to other people who were going through hard times.

And that's basically what's happened in my life. These opportunities keep coming up, and you try and jump at them.

Memorable Moment

In 1994 the program I was with was bought out, and the new owners didn't have a place for me. I was at a race in Portland and a writer-friend came up to me and said, "I've got an opportunity for you."

I said, "Oh? What's that?"

He said, "How'd you like to be chief steward?"

I looked at him and smiled and said, "I know *who* the chief steward is, but I don't know *what* he is or does."

He said, "Well, you've got an interview with Andrew Craig [CEO of Championship Auto Racing Teams] in two hours." He had it all organized for me.

So I got the rule book out of my toolbox, read what a chief steward was, and went down to this interview.

I got in there, and this gentleman was pretty vibrant and very excited about the direction he wanted to go. Throughout that year we had several conversations and did some more interviews. The chief steward's job is a high-profile job. The people who have done it before have always been drivers. Wally Dallenbach, Sr., has done it for fourteen years. It's a position elected by the board of directors, who are all the car owners.

When I got into it and realized what it was all about, I saw it was a no-win situation. There were too many obstacles in the way and too many requirements to fulfill.

Still, partway through, every hurdle put in front of me, every barrier, just melted away. It just continued to happen. I went for my final interview with Andrew, and afterward Andrew looked at me and said, "You're the man. You're the one I want to do this job. Let's figure out how we're going to make this happen." And we did.

It's the most exciting, most demanding, and most difficult job I've ever done in my life. I enjoy it. There's certainly some grief. You're always the bad guy, because when you police twenty-eight competitors, you will never make all twenty-eight of them happy. There will always be at least one you've made angry.

But there have also been lots of opportunities to witness to people. They present themselves all the time. It's the direction I've chosen, and I'm enjoying it a lot and it's a lot of fun. And it's still *very* challenging.

LAKE SPEED

Driver/General Manager
#9
Spam
Harry Melling Racing Ford Thunderbird

Lake Speed is the very model of dogged determination. For years, he's worked his way up through the ranks of drivers, always driving well for underfunded, overworked teams. He's been equally determined in his pursuit of a team that reflects his unshakable Christian faith and value system.

Today, as he nears fifty, Lake and his wife, Rice (pronounced Ree–sa), are the first couple of the Christian community in NASCAR. They've persevered with both their reputation and witness intact and opened their home to a thousand and one lonely, lost crew members and drivers needing a good meal and the Word of God.

While the aquamarine/turquoise #9 Spam car hasn't won in a couple of years, strong ownership from Harry Melling and Lake's driving skills have made sure it's always competitive, always in the hunt. And each time it howls around the track, a silent prayer of thanks and blessing goes up from at least one person in each and every pit it passes.

When you touch that many lives, it always comes back to you a hundredfold.

At the age of fifteen, I was baptized and joined a church. I figured I was saved, I had my ticket to heaven, and I could go on my merry way. I knew my Bible verses and went to church every Sunday and did what I wanted the rest of the week. I even took three semesters of Bible in the Christian college I attended. But I never put the whole picture together.

I didn't think about it again until I was leading the race at Talladega in May of 1983, with about ten to twelve laps left to go. I was on the backstretch when a small voice spoke to me right quick, a voice I'd never heard before. "Lake, what are you going to do if you win here too?"

Now, stock car racing is as tough a competition as you'll find anywhere on God's green earth. In the beginning, I had serious doubts about competing because I had no contacts or financial support and wasn't part of the racing clique. But there I was, leading a race, after starting from scratch on the NASCAR circuit in 1980.

When I heard that voice, it really shook me up. It was similar to an experience I'd had in 1978 at the Le Mans racetrack in France when I won the World's Championship of Karting. I'd spent nineteen years in kart racing and when I won the world's championship, the only non-European to ever do it, I thought, *Well, now what?*

I still remember standing on the winner's podium at Le Mans with all of the noise of the celebration and suddenly realizing there was only one person I really knew at the race. I thought, *What is this all for?* I was so focused on racing and was so self-centered that my wife had divorced me and I'd lost my son.

I remembered all of this at Talladega when I heard that questioning voice.

I had a bad pit stop near the end of the race and eventually finished third. Afterward, I thought a lot about my life. I was going back to an apartment, not a house. I was going back to a live-in girlfriend, not a family. Racing was good and fun, but it wouldn't last forever. And did people really love Lake Speed or just love what he did? All of a sudden, my life looked pretty shallow.

I started asking myself some questions about life. Where was the truth in the world that you could really sink your teeth into?

The little voice came to me again and said, "There is a Book that has been around thousands of years that some of the evilest, meanest people in history have tried to overrule—but it's still around. If you want to know the truth, try reading the Bible."

After Talladega, my girlfriend, Rice, and I sat on the edge of the bed and started reading the Bible. Our relationship was as worldly and as crazy as it could be. I was racing all over the country and, if she didn't come with me, I had other girlfriends. She had her friends when I wasn't around too. Both of us played the same game and neither one was getting anywhere.

When we started reading the Bible, it didn't take us long to realize that God really loved us. But He also had ways for us to live our lives, things not to do—a lot of which we did on a regular basis—things that smelled good, tasted good, and felt good!

That was in May 1983, and we began to read and go to church on a regular basis when I wasn't racing. Rice was a research nurse at the time and some of the ladies at her clinic invited us to attend their church. We went to the church, which was sort of on the other side of the tracks and pretty rough compared to the church we had been going to.

It was a different experience from any I had ever had in church. I was used to things being real solemn and reverent. These folks were having a great time. It was like a party. They were all singing and happy. Yet these people were serious. It was the first time I'd been in a church service where people really worshiped the Lord. I felt really strange, but I began to recognize the Spirit I'd been reading about in the New Testament.

The pastor made an altar call and asked, "Is there anyone here who wants to turn his or her life over to the Lord Jesus Christ?"

I heard that little voice again saying, "Lake, you wanted to know the truth, what life was all about. You've been running your own life since you were twenty-three years old. You've made a mess out of it, chasing material things that were here today and gone tomorrow. Why don't you turn your life over to Me and let Me guide you?"

Boy, I tell you, tears came down my face and I made a decision right there. I said, "I'm tired of trying to figure out how to be happy and successful. I can't do it. I'm ready to let You try."

As I left that pew to make a confession of my faith, I heard another voice screaming at me: "If you go down front, you will never race again!"

I said, "I don't care if I ever race again. I'm going to give the Lord a try."

Since I was a little kid, I always thought that if you were a dynamite, committed Christian, you went to Africa or somewhere as a missionary to teach pygmies. So I went down front totally believing that I would never race again.

I was willing to put my faith in the Lord when I made that altar call. And because I was willing to totally give up racing, God gave it back to me. The Lord said that I'd always raced for me, now I was to race for Him. He gave me the unique talent to race so I would witness and testify for the Lord from the platform of racing. I could do more for the Lord this way than I could ever do trying to win a pygmy over or handing out religious tracts on a street corner.

The Holy Spirit speaks very loudly at times and really stops me in my tracks. I had one of the foulest mouths imaginable, and that was one of the things that the Lord cleaned up instantly. In my new nature, it just wasn't acceptable anymore.

My real prayer life began when I went down front and prayed and asked the Lord Jesus Christ to save my soul. From that day forward, I knew that I could speak to Him and hear Him.

Memorable Moment

In 1985, a first-class NASCAR racing team that won four races the year before asked me to be their new driver, but they didn't have a sponsor.

Rice and I had been married in 1984. She'd had the same experience in that little church. We both prayed to know whether we should leave Jackson, Mississippi, where we had our roots and families, and move to Charlotte, North Carolina, to join the team. I never, ever thought I would leave Jackson. My dad had been mayor there and it was home.

But we felt the Lord was leading us. It would give me a greater opportunity to continue the talks and testimony I gave about how my life had changed through Christ. It would also be a giant leap of faith to join a new team without a sponsor in a new town.

We prayed and prayed . . . and then we packed up and moved. We trusted God that we had made the right decision.

As the team prepared for the racing season, Rice and I prayed every day for a sponsor. I often read from Isaiah 41:13, "For I, the

LORD your God, will hold your right hand, / Saying to you, 'Fear not, I will help you.'"

For several months, I helped the team owners, calling people, having meetings, and doing everything I could to get money. It was discouraging, but several times I heard that voice say, "Lake, why don't you trust Me?"

The Daytona 500 is the Super Bowl of stock car racing and is the first race of the season. The team was running out of money and no sponsor had appeared. We decided to race anyway. If the team had to shut down after Daytona, so be it.

Sometimes teams arrange for partial sponsorship at races. Usually these are associate sponsors who get their names on a small part of the race car for just the one race. We practiced and then qualified for the race with our car, a plain white car with a big blue number—and no sponsor's name.

Saturday, I was watching a preliminary race from the Goodyear Tires hospitality suite in the stands. A man I had briefly met in the garage area sat next to me. His name was Kent Brown and he said, "I've never been to a stock car race before. Can you tell me what's going on?"

I said, "Oh, boy! You've got a real treat in store!"

The race started and all of the cars were running real close. The pit stops were quick. A car spun out. And this guy was getting real excited. He wouldn't leave my side!

When the race was over, he said, "This is the most exciting thing I've ever seen. I'm with Nationwide Auto Parts. I came here to work out a sponsorship with a team, but I've never been able to connect with them. Would y'all be interested in an associate sponsor?"

Sunday I started the Daytona 500 with the painted-on sponsor's name still wet on the car! The team owners told Kent Brown they were so grateful for his signing on as an associate sponsor for the year that they put his company's name on the car just as if he were a full sponsor.

What racing gives Lake Speed is competition. I enjoy trying to beat other teams, getting my car to run a little better, a little faster. To outrun competitors who have more funding and depth in their racing equipment just tickles me to death. That Sunday I

■ 21 ■

finished second at Daytona to Bill Elliott, who went on to win a lot of races that year!

I was driving into the garage area after the race and the first guy I saw was Kent Brown. He was completely unglued. "This is great! This is wonderful! We're not going to take our company name off your car. Don't worry about sponsorship. I'll get the money somehow. We'll sponsor you fully for the rest of the year."

I was elated and as I got out of my car, the TV cameras, instead of staying with the winner in Victory Lane, turned to me. A guy came over and stuck a microphone in front of me. Everyone knew that we'd come to Daytona with no sponsor.

He said, "Lake, this is great! You've finished second! What does this mean to you?"

There were a lot of people around me, hugging and celebrating, but at that very noisy instant, I heard this little voice say, "I told you so, Lake. I told you that I'd do it."

I burst into tears and started bawling like a baby. I don't remember what I said, but I thanked the Lord for giving me a good run and answering my prayers.

I flew to New York to be on *Good Morning America* and we got a lot of publicity. Most people thought I was emotional because I finished second. That didn't have anything to do with it. It was the answered prayer that moved me.

Prayer is going before the Lord and just communicating with Him. I talk to the Lord in my consciousness, or verbally. Sometimes I sing. Sometimes I holler.

I think God cries over those who don't pray. I really do. I think God wants a relationship with people. If you care deeply about your wife or your children and all of a sudden they don't communicate with you, it hurts. God is deeply hurt when we, as His children, deny Him and turn our backs on Him.

God chuckles a lot when He looks at me. "Here's ol' Lake; he's really messed up again. He tries hard, but he still stumbles. I have to pick him up now and then and dust him off. But he's still trying."

I used to party and play and have a big ol' time. But I'm here to tell you I have a whole lot more fun now. I don't have a guilty conscience or hangovers anymore. I'm really enjoying my new life with the Lord.

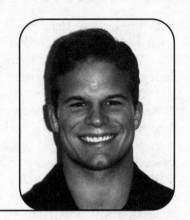

MARCUS SMITH

Sales and Marketing
Charlotte Motor Speedway

It's not easy for any son living in his father's shadow, particularly if that shadow is cast by O. Burton Smith, the most powerful man in NASCAR. But Marcus Smith is doing just fine, thank you. The handsome, engaging son of the owner of the Charlotte, Atlanta, and new Dallas-Fort Worth speedways has found his niche, combining his love of the sport with an active, heartfelt Christian faith.

My younger brother and I were in the Good News Club when I was about six. We learned the verses and stories and songs. One day the teacher told us more about salvation. Toward the end, the instructor said, "If anyone would like to stay after and invite Jesus into his or her heart, meet me in the kitchen."

My brother, David (no relation to David Smith, page 145) said, "I want to do that. Come on, let's go do that."

I said, "No, Mom's waiting for us. Let's go."

I really didn't think much of it, but he said, "Well, I'm going to do it."

So I went with him. I can still picture it. There was a wooden table with the wooden chairs with the rods on the back. We sat around the table and prayed and asked Jesus into our hearts. From then on I knew that, yes, I was a Christian. That's pretty much what I knew about it—that I was going to heaven.

We went to church not necessarily every week, but on a sort of regular basis. We were in Sunday school.

My parents got separated when I was fifteen, but after that the Lord just brought me around somehow. Dan Young was the Young Life leader for our high school. Dan would always come to our wrestling matches and our football games and I'd see him at the basketball games. Some of my friends went to Young Life, so I started to go in tenth grade.

My mother, during the whole separation, began to really cling to God. She would tell us about her prayers and how they had been answered and how certain verses in the Bible were special to her. Verses like Romans 8:28: "And we know that all things work together for good to those who love God, to those who are the called according to His purpose." And James 5:16: "The effective, fervent prayer of a righteous man avails much."

She would tell us stories about how she would pray for us. It was kind of a nasty divorce and she prayed that things would work out well. And people came out of the woodwork, people we really didn't know that well but who loved us so much they let us stay in their homes for weeks. It was really amazing. When I look back on it, that had a big effect on me—the love that was shown to us.

The summer before my junior year I went to Saranac Young Life Camp in New York on Lake Saranac. I had pretty much decided in my own mind by then that I wanted to be a Christian. I wanted to be on fire for God, but I didn't really know that much. I wasn't reading my Bible all that much although I was in a Young Life Bible study.

I hadn't verbally recommitted my life to God yet. At camp there was a speaker the Lord really moved. I felt like the Lord was speaking to me through him. His name was Greg Leisinger and he was a great guy. He was the emcee for the two weeks that we were there.

Toward the end of the camp, they had a night to go out alone and make a decision. They said, "Go out, have time alone. Don't go with your girlfriend, don't go with your buddies. Just go out and spend time with God and think about some of this stuff."

I sat on the back porch steps of the cabin, kind of overlooking the lake. It was a beautiful night, and I just poured my heart out to the Lord. I recommitted my life to Him. I told Him I wanted to live for Him, that I loved Him.

Over the next couple of days, as I read my Bible, it talked about making a confession to others. I thought, *Wow. I need to do that, too.* I was really worried about this, but finally that night I told all the guys in my cabin that I was a Christian, that I had made that commitment the night before, and that was the way I was going to live. That's when I recommitted my life to Him publicly.

After that, college was a big decision for me. I'd prayed about it and really at first I didn't want to go to North Carolina at Chapel Hill because around here, almost everybody goes there. I had an opportunity to go to Wheaton College and I thought, *How could I go wrong there? God sure must want me to go there; it's one of the best Christian schools in the world.* I could have had a scholarship and been a star on the wrestling team there. But my mother and I kept praying for God to open and close the doors.

In the end, things went great for Carolina. We decided that's where I'd go. And it worked out great. I had an awesome time.

Initially, I was worried about not having Christian fellowship, but two of the incoming freshman wrestlers were also Christians. We started praying together. Other guys came to the Lord through that. Then I got active in Athletes in Action and InterVarsity Christian Fellowship. We had a great time there, too.

When I first started school, I thought I was going be a doctor. But I didn't like science, so that didn't work. My dad had a few businesses, and I thought I would try one of those. Eventually, I chose the Speedway.

I wasn't sure about it, though, until about two years ago at the Coca–Cola 600. We had the MRO chapel service down in the garage. Franklin Graham spoke and afterward he came up to our suite. I talked to him for a little bit, and he asked me what I was planning to do after college. I said, "Well, I'm not really sure. I've thought about going into the ministry, I've thought about going into medicine, I've even thought about the Speedway and staying here."

And he said, "Wow, it sure would be neat to see a man like you in a place like this—a godly influence in a facility like Charlotte Motor Speedway."

That confirmed to me that God was saying, "Marcus, you can serve Me outside the ministry." I knew that was what I wanted to do.

That was a big turning point in my life. After that, I changed my track from medicine to marketing and learned more about what goes on in the business world. I really enjoyed it.

After graduation, when I first started working at the Speedway, that is, inside the building (I'd picked up trash in the yard and that kind of thing before), one of the neatest things I've experienced was gathering with a few other people and starting to pray that God would use the Speedway in some way for His glory. We also prayed for people and things that were going on in the Speedway.

Then, somehow, we got together with Bob Dyar in MRO and he said they'd been praying about the same thing! It seems that another Christian organization had contacted them and they wanted a contact with the Speedway. So that was our first bite. We thought it was great. When that didn't pan out, we kept praying about it and we were contacted by Promise Keepers. *They* contacted *us*. We didn't go anywhere or ask anyone, we just prayed and left it in God's hands. Nothing would have happened without God.

I got married June 8, 1996, and we went on our honeymoon. I got back on a Friday afternoon at 4:30. The plane landed and I drove toward the Speedway. And as I was driving out, on the radio at 6:30 came the live Promise Keepers broadcast! The announcer said, "Live from Charlotte Motor Speedway, Promise Keepers '96!"

I was so overwhelmed with real joy that these prayers for the past four years had come to fruition. It was awesome. This was a Promise Keepers conference with about fifty-five thousand guys here. Next year they want to do even more here.

Memorable Moment

My most memorable moment has been seeing how God has brought this sport so far. Seeing Jeff Gordon and Bobby Hillin coming back from Michigan just for Promise Keepers—for them to stand up and tell fifty-five thousand guys, plus all the radio and TV audience, that they love the Lord, they're not ashamed of it, and

He's what they live for. Afterward Jeff said, "Man, I've won all kinds of races and done all kinds of things, but that's the best thing I've ever done."

And that's topped it all for me so far.

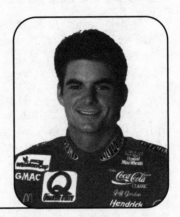

JEFF GORDON

Driver
#24
Rick Hendrick Motorsport
DuPont Automotive Finishes Chevrolet Monte Carlo

What's left to say about Jeff Gordon? Jeff's 1995 (seven wins, nine poles, most bonuses, and season's earnings of more than $4.3 million) would still seem slightly unreal if he hadn't followed it with a more impressive 1996 (ten victories, second in the points standings, with a whopping $2,484,518 earned). The result is that the young, handsome Gordon and his beautiful wife, Brooke, are the reigning king and queen of NASCAR's Camelot.

Jeff's rapid rise to the top is already the stuff legends are made of; he

- *began racing in the powerful, dangerous sprint cars at age thirteen.*
- *was 1991's Busch Grand National Series Rookie of the Year.*
- *was 1993's MAXX Rookie of the Year, fourteenth in the point standings.*
- *was eighth in the Winston Cup standings in 1994, including wins at the inaugural Brickyard 400 and the Coca-Cola 600.*
- *was, in 1995 at age twenty-four, the second youngest driver in history to win NASCAR's Winston Cup.*

The sky's obviously the limit for the humble, soft-spoken Indiana native. But in this case, the sky features #24's brilliant rainbow of colors!

I didn't grow up in a church. I may have gone to a church a half-dozen times that I can remember in my life. My mom and my father got divorced when I was just one. My stepfather and my mother married shortly after that and so that's kind of the main relationship that I've had, being with them.

I came from a family who spent a lot of time racing—ever since I was five years old. I've been racing every weekend since I can remember. Church never really was a part of it until recently—I'd say within the last five years.

The neat thing about Winston Cup racing is that they bring the church to you—and that's through Max Helton and Motor Racing Outreach. Before I was in NASCAR, I was racing in the Busch Grand National level and they started to bring the church into that. It was there that I started getting interested in it.

Later, I started to see some drivers like Darrell Waltrip, Bobby Hillin, Lake Speed, Mark Martin, and others that were going to the Winston Cup chapel. I was obviously wanting to be a Winston Cup driver, so I started going to the church services. I found it very interesting and discovered a way I wanted to live my life. At the time I wasn't a picture-perfect child. I was doing some things that were kind of out on the edge, living life dangerously. But once I got to know Christ, I'll tell you what, it helped me be a better person. I think it helped me make better decisions about my life and also about my career. My life's never been better since.

Brooke has had a big influence on me. She grew up in a Christian family and went to private schools and studied the Bible all through school. So she educated me a lot because I had a lot of questions about things I wanted to know more about, and our talks helped me to grow closer to Jesus. She was a huge influence on me and somebody who taught me a lot. I feel like God brought her to me. She's my angel. I feel we were put together for a reason.

The one moment that I felt was more powerful than any other was when Brooke and I got engaged. I decided to get baptized—something that I'd never done before—at the church she, her mother, and her grandmother were baptized in. Her whole family goes to this church, a little tiny one in North Carolina. I went up there and the whole way I'm thinking, *Well, I'm finally going to get baptized—no big deal.* But that experience was one of the most thrilling, exhilarating experiences that I've ever had! I came out of that water and felt like a new person. I felt something just so strong inside of me, it almost brought tears to my eyes. It was such a great feeling. It was like winning the biggest race ever.

Ever since then, the Spirit has been very strong inside me. And since then, we spend more time in Bible studies, asking a lot more questions.

It's funny, but when I first started going to church, I would be thinking, *Boy, this is really long—the services take a long time.* But now I feel like it just flies by because I'm more interested in what's being said. There are so many things about the Bible that are true in everyday life, but when you look back at the historical records, you say, "Man, that really happened! These things really took place! It's amazing!"

Since becoming a Christian, I think I'm much more content with life. When I make a decision, whether it is on the racetrack or in business off the racetrack, I feel good about what I'm doing, no matter what. I know I'm not perfect. I ask for forgiveness for many things all the time. But where it shows the most, I think, is in the contentment I feel. This is true whether I finish thirty-first on that racetrack or whether I'm in the Winner's Circle praising God. I praise God just as much for thirty-first or thirty-fifth as I do for winning.

I now feel like life has a whole lot more meaning than just winning or losing on the racetrack. There are so many more things about it, so many more beautiful places to go than just Victory Lane! If I know and feel that in my heart, I'm going to make better decisions and think about things a little bit differently from how I would before.

You chose the rainbow for your team colors. Is there any spiritual significance to that choice?

No, not really. The rainbow came because the paint company—basically I'm sponsored by Du Pont Automotive Finishes—

wanted a spectrum of colors. Then, because we carry a tomahawk over our pits, we were named "The Rainbow Warriors."

But one thing I do every weekend is carry a Scripture from the Bible that usually Brooke picks out or we pick out together. Usually it is something that might have to do with that particular track. That might be a real difficult track, or a track where there is usually a lot of contact or a lot of accidents, so we'll maybe have a verse that has something about "shields" or "strengthen me"—things like that. That is in the car every single weekend. Other drivers do that too. I think we learned it from Darrell Waltrip and his wife, Stevie. Now I don't know what I'd do if I didn't have a Scripture on the steering wheel.

Memorable Moment

I'd have to say the Brickyard 400, the inaugural one in 1994—winning that race was that moment. The Brickyard 400 not only accelerated my career, but I think it accelerated my relationship with God as well because I wanted that race so bad. Before the race and during the race, I was praying every spare moment that I got. I was whispering prayers like, "Lord, You know I need You badly. This is such a big race to me and I want it so badly. I've got the car, I've got the team, I've got everything it takes—if I could just have You on my side also, I know that I can win this race!" And He answered my prayers. I'll never forget that. I think it was one way that has actually helped me grow stronger within Him also. Be careful what you pray for!

JOHN DODSON

Mechanic

#10

Tide

Rudd Performance Motorsports Ford Thunderbird

John and Kelly Dodson look like a storybook couple, the kind of attractive young people you see advertising Tide detergent on TV. Actually, John's been around a while. Fans of the late, lamented Blue Max team will remember him as one of the trio of Dodson brothers (along with Barry and Brad) who helped Rusty Wallace take the checkered flag sixteen times in four years.

What they probably don't know is that it was John who rallied the devastated Dodson family when Barry lost his two children in a car crash outside Darlington, South Carolina.

The memories of Barry's pain and loss remained fresh in John's mind. Shortly thereafter, John asked owner/driver Ricky Rudd and crew chief Richard Broome if he could rotate off the travel team to spend more time with Kelly and their growing family. Both men graciously agreed.

Each weekend the entire Dodson clan now gathers around the television to root vigorously for the orange/red/yellow Tide car together!

I didn't really come from a Christian background. Instead, my wife, Kelly, had a lot to do with my coming to a personal relationship with Jesus Christ. In 1996, we'll have been married for twelve years, and in that time she's been my strength. She's taught me a lot about the Lord, and she's answered a lot of questions for me. She was raised in a Christian family. Her father has taught me a whole lot as well. At the racetrack, MRO has helped also.

Kelly and I were married when we were very young—I was twenty-two and she was twenty. We moved to the Charlotte area the same year and went off on our own.

How it all came about was, Kelly had been baptized when she was younger, but she wanted to be baptized again in a church near Mooresville when I quit traveling with the team (I don't go on the road anymore). So as she started talking about that, I went with her to talk to our pastor. He asked me if I'd like to be baptized too. Kelly and I had talked about it ahead of time and I told her that I would, but I thought I had never become a born-again Christian.

In this span of our marriage, Kelly had already explained so much to me and answered so many questions. Still, honestly, I was pretty ignorant. In praying by myself, I'd asked the Lord to forgive me, and I'd asked the Lord to come into my life. This much I'd learned from listening to Christian radio. I'd prayed the Sinner's Prayer with the evangelists.

That day our preacher asked me if I'd ever prayed that prayer. I said, "Yes."

Then he said, "Well then, you are saved."

Nothing had ever really rung a bell before. But when I was baptized shortly thereafter, when I came out of that tank, it changed my life. I *felt* it. I felt contentment. I felt freedom. I felt happiness. And I felt hunger to learn more.

Today, my radio stays on a Christian station. I keep a Bible in my toolbox, and I can read Scripture anytime I want during my workday. I want to hear good preaching. I want to learn more and more. There's so much I want to learn.

That's the way I feel I have changed. Any problems we have, we just let the Lord handle them, as best we can. As the Lord leads you, just lay your problems on Him—that's what I have found has worked best for me. I'm not as anxious as I used to be—I used to be a workaholic. I still stay very busy, but I've found that you need to save time for your family life. You need to put God first in your family—and everything else falls right into place. It *all* falls right into place.

At work, I feel like you have to be careful to witness to people. That's something that's hard for me to do. I really tiptoe around it. There's a fine line you can cross there. But I want to let people know.

I also got my contractor's license, and I'm building my first home. I let people I hire know that I'm a Christian. I don't expect anything out of them; I just want them to know going in. I want the people that I work with to know it. I don't want to hear the unnecessary language. I don't want to hear any whining. Let's just stay positive.

I don't think a lot of people are ready to accept it, especially in the racing industry. There are so many people from so many different places in it, but there are as many people who *do* want to hear it as there are people who do not. A lot of them you can talk to. But I don't press the issue. I never start it; I always wait for an opening. And if you keep that Bible in your toolbox, people know it. I keep a few verses around my workplace too.

Memorable Moment

It would have to be the day we won the Winston Cup Championship with my brothers Barry and Brad. We were Blue Max racing, and Rusty Wallace was our driver in 1989. For six years we'd been trying to attain this goal. And when it all came together, that final moment, I just lost it. I couldn't control my emotions anymore. I just wept out loud.

And now that I look back on it, winning was a small thing. In racing it was something we'd fought for for years. But you really had to give to attain it; you had to give too much to get to that point. You deprive your family, you deprive the Lord, you deprive a whole lot of people to get to that goal. I just don't see how anybody who is ultrasuccessful can do it. There *are* people who can do it when they're 100 percent with the Lord. But then there are people who do it who are 5 percent with the Lord, and they do it by depriving everyone else in their lives.

If you'll keep your priorities in order, you can obtain anything. If people want to obtain fame through racing, they'll obtain it. I could have become a crew chief. Anything you want to be, I think you can do that.

But do I want to travel thirty-two weekends a year, plus testing, leaving my family here alone? And when my little girl's eighteen and going to college, do I want to sit there thinking, *Man, I wish I'd spent more time at home?* I'm not going to do it. The Lord came into my life shortly after she was born. I got off the road soon after that.

Racing's a big thing and winning that championship was great, but an hour after it's over, it's history. It means a lot and it has given me longevity in the sport, but it's just a trophy you can put on the wall. It means nothing to me compared to my family and God.

I don't want this to sound wrong—I'm just saying that success in racing is wonderful, but it's not going to get you into heaven and it's not going to determine how you raise your family. That's my number-one job: being a daddy and a husband. That's the way I look at it. I have the best time right here in my home, more than anyplace I can travel to.

We won sixteen races in four years. But you win a race and you start over again on Monday. It happens so fast in this sport that you hardly have time to think about it before you're at another race. You can't celebrate too long. We got to where we'd won so many times, we were thinking once we got into Victory Lane, *Let's get this deal over with. I'm ready to go home. I'm tired.*

Time goes so fast. You don't have time to go to the chapel services at the track when you're going day and night like that. You don't have time for anything.

JEFF CHANDLER

Mechanic/Race Day Front-Tire Changer
#18
Interstate Batteries
Joe Gibbs Racing Monte Carlo

Jeff Chandler is the excitable sort. He can wax positively poetic talking about #18's 358-cubic-inch V-8 that develops 730 horsepower at 8,000 RPM. He can rave on and on about the courage of driver Bobby Labonte, the skill of crew chief Jimmy Makar, the charisma of owner Joe Gibbs. And he still gets animated when describing how Jesus Christ came into his life!

Jeff is a key ingredient in the composition of the lime-green machine's consistent success on NASCAR tracks across the country. Need more proof? His peers named him All-Pro Tire Changer in 1994.

I was raised in a Catholic home, and I always thought I was a Christian. But in 1995, I'd already been in Winston Cup–type racing for ten years, and I'd got into the whole partying-hard, staying-out-late-nights type of stuff. But about a year ago, I felt like I'd hit an all-time low.

It was the week after the Brickyard 500 in Indianapolis and I saw Bob Dyar from Motor Racing Outreach. It was raining at Watkins Glen, New York, so we had a lot of time on our hands. We struck up a conversation because I knew there had to be a better way than the way I was living. Bob gave me a couple of books to read that explained the gospel, about what Jesus actually did for you. They also pointed out the verses in the Bible that say you cannot come to heaven unless you come through Jesus Christ. I'd never really thought about that before.

What I read made me realize what Jesus Christ actually did, what He went through for each and every one of us. The books also said that no matter how many good works you do, you're still not going to measure up to the expectations of God, so you have to have Jesus Christ. No matter how good we are, we *still* have to have Jesus Christ to get us into heaven. Those books went through that entire process, step-by-step.

Within a seven-day period, I read one of the books straight through. At the end of that week, I was sitting in a motel room in Dover, Delaware. My roommate was getting ready to go out to the bars, and he asked me if I was going. For the first time, I said, "I think I'm going to hang here at the room tonight."

When I finished the book, I asked Jesus Christ to be my personal Savior. I know He answered my prayer.

I quit drinking that night, and I haven't had a drink since. Everything's been going real well. It's made my relationship with my wife and children a thousand times better.

My relationships at work are different too. I was working at another shop at the time and those guys were out every night we were on the road. Everybody said, "What's wrong with you? Why won't you go out with us?" They didn't understand. I finally said, "I believe I don't want to do that anymore."

When they kept asking me questions, I realized I didn't have all of the answers because I'd never read the Bible. At home, we didn't have Bible study—we didn't read the Bible. I was raised to think that I was going to heaven. But now, looking back on it, I'm not so sure if I was or not. I'm real sure of it now because I have come to know the Lord and it's a great thing.

Coming to work for Joe Gibbs was unbelievable because I accepted Christ before I came to work for him. Not a month after I accepted Christ, this opportunity arose. I thought, *This team provides a better atmosphere for a young Christian than the atmosphere I was in*. I felt that I was at the point where I needed to be in a better atmosphere, be around stronger Christians, because I felt even then that I could still be swayed back and forth.

Joe has Bible studies every week. First and foremost, he'll tell you he's trying to promote the Lord. So it has worked out real good for me. I talk to the Lord regularly now.

Memorable Moment

In racing, I've been really fortunate. Maybe not by some people's standards, but by mine I've been fairly successful. I've been in Victory Lane in the Winston Cup five times. I was a crew chief on a Busch car when we won three fairly large races with Michael Waltrip. We sat on the pole at Daytona, won Charlotte, won Bristol, won Darlington in a ten-week span. I've had a lot of success with that.

The other event I remember came after I'd already asked the Lord to come into my life. He was working with me because I was having a lot of trouble, a lot of peaks and valleys. About then, we went to Charlotte Motor Speedway for the race. I'm considered one of the best in my field when it comes to changing tires. But we'd made two or three pit stops during the race and I hadn't had a good pit stop yet. I kept thinking, *What's wrong?* So I kept telling myself, "You're the best, you can do it." But every time I'd go out there, I'd fall flat on my face. I wasn't getting the job done.

So it was midway through the race, when you *have* to perform. If we wanted a chance to win, I had to do my job. When they pulled into the pit, I looked at the race car coming down pit road and I looked up and I said, "Okay, Jesus. I'm not getting the job done. You come do it for me . . . and I'm just going to go along for the ride."

And it was almost like an out-of-body experience. I can remember watching myself change the tires, but not actually doing it. It was the fastest pit stop I've ever done in my life. When I finished, I thought, *I didn't do that. I just sat there and watched it happening. I didn't really do that!* Then I realized the Lord came down and did it for me. He just let me go along for the ride.

So that's become a habit for me. Every time I get ready to make a pit stop, I just ask the Lord to come down and do it for me. And I've become a better tire-changer for all of it, too.

The most memorable victory, though, was two years ago at

Loudon, New Hampshire, with Ricky Rudd. It was a new team. Everybody said we couldn't start a new team and yet, within the first half of a season, we'd won our first major race! We took the lead with twelve laps to go and passed Dale Earnhardt on the outside to do it! Rusty was running third, Jeff Gordon was fourth—we had all of the heavy hitters right there, so it wasn't like we were backing into it. We passed Earnhardt and all of the guys were standing on the wall, cheering Rusty on.

But I walked to the back of the pits and sat on a stack of tires by myself. At that point I hadn't yet committed my life to the Lord, but I can remember thanking Him for letting us win that race because even then I knew that the Lord was providing that for us. I was actually in a kind of seclusion in the back of the pit when we won.

So God was dealing with you before you even knew it.

I think He's been dealing with me for a long time. Looking back, there have been a lot of positive influences. My first Christian encounter came with Darrell Waltrip and it was at the time Darrell was just coming to the Lord. I knew Darrell before and I remember looking at Darrell and thinking, *This guy, he's no Christian. I know what he's done.* But now that I've become a Christian, I can look at that and say it's a good thing there's forgiveness! Because I was just as bad, if not worse, than anybody out there. Thank God for forgiveness.

CHARLEY PRESSLEY

Crew Chief
#41
Larry Hedrick Motorsports
Kodiak Racing Monte Carlo

It's like pulling teeth to get Charley Pressley to talk about himself. If you want to talk about the car under the distinctive snarling Kodiak bear logo, he'll talk all day. Or if you want to talk about his driver, Ricky Craven, he'll bend your ear. He'll happily mention his wife, Alison, or his brother, Robert Pressley. And he's always delighted to talk about his father, former racing star Bob Pressley, and how he once won thirty-five out of fifty-two races on the Busch circuit. But himself, no.

Still, if you're patient, Charley will eventually share a little about his life and faith. If you're not alert, the conversation will quickly divert to the people he's worked with—Tim Richmond, Morgan Shepherd, Leo Jackson, and others.

As a result, it's a lot easier to get other people to talk about Charley Pressley. To wit:

"Charley fits right into our scheme as we continue to make moves which we feel will strengthen our team. He definitely will complement our efforts."—Owner Larry Hedrick

"I've got a lot of confidence in Charley, in his abilities as well as his experience. He knows the sport, the people, and has the knowledge to help us bring a lot of things together that will make our team more competitive."—Driver Ricky Craven

He couldn't—and wouldn't—have said it better himself!

Growing up, I spent a lot time with my grandparents. They were very devout in the church. My father has been in racing forever; he started when I was about eight years old. He was a driver and raced on Sunday. But every week we went to Sunday school and he was always sitting there waiting for us when we got out, and then we went racing.

My first experience with Jesus Christ was early on—five, six, seven years old. It came from going to Sunday school and being exposed to Christian things, as well as going to church with Grandma and Grandpa. Because of my background, I've made commitments, looking back now, two or three different times. I knew God, but then I wandered off, going astray for a while. All the distractions that can happen, happened. But I'm on the journey back now.

How does your faith impact your life?

It's really helping me in all aspects. I'm forty years old now, so I can look back to when I was fourteen or so and see that I had a strong relationship even then. I can look back now and see how He influenced my life so much, how good things really were back then.

When I became the seventeen-, eighteen-year-old with freedom, out on my own, that's when I really messed it up. I let the distractions distract me. It's taken me many years to get back. I would go back for a while. Like everybody else, you get desperate and turn back to Him. Then you get going again, thinking, *Well, I pulled myself out of it again*, so you start neglecting Him. Motorsports probably don't offer any distractions that aren't there for the everyday working guy.

Since so much of what you do is on Sunday, how do you stay strong in the Word?

Well, there have been many, many people, places, and ministries that have helped me for years. My grandparents loved Billy Graham. So every time he's on, I dial him in. I also attribute some of the credit to TV preacher Gene Scott in California for helping bring me back in line, although I know to some, he's probably a little radical. About 1980 or 1981, I was in a motel room at a racetrack. I'd been out drinking and came in late at night and I turned the TV on. I wasn't watching it, but I was hearing something. I thought it might be *Saturday Night Live* or some comedy program.

When I finally tuned in, a guy was sitting there in a big fur coat and a cowboy hat with a big cigar. I heard him preach a little bit. Then I heard him say something, like Father Guido Sarducci might say on *Saturday Night Live*. It was Gene Scott.

The next day at the track I said, "Did you guys hear this Gene Scott person? Who *is* this guy?" It was amazing.

I had a satellite system put in at my home and the first thing that popped up when I got back was Gene Scott! I listened to him for days. And that's really when my life began to turn back around.

In August 1995, I was without a job, so I turned to God even more then. I found a little church close to home, a small Baptist country church. It's always been very rewarding. I miss being there Sunday. Our current work structure only permits me maybe to go home on Wednesday nights now and catch at least the Wednesday night service. But when I'm home, I go. I also listen to a lot of Christian radio.

Memorable Moment

There have been many of them. Especially with my father, growing up and racing with him. I remember him winning the state championship one year. I was very proud of him. I was probably thirteen or fourteen years old. I was a part of it.

Then in 1977 and 1978, he ran for a championship again and we finished second. That was rewarding. We wanted to win, obviously, but it was still rewarding to finish second.

And in racing, the thing that most left a loss and a void was the death of Davey Allison. I'd become good friends with him. Another shocker was Ernie Irvan's horrible accident. That was one where I prayed hard. I didn't want to hear how bad he was. I just refused to accept that I was going to lose another friend.

The most recent near-tragedy was with Ricky Craven and his wreck at Talladega. That was stunning, a shock to us all. But he survived. I was there with Ricky and I got to see him. When I saw him in the hospital, his eyes were open and he was at least responding to something. It was only then that I knew everything else could be worked out.

PHIL PARSONS

Driver/Co–Owner

#10

CHANNELLOCK Racing

Phil Parsons Racing Chevrolet Monte Carlo

There are few more distinctive cars on the Busch Grand National Stock Car circuit than the blue CHANNELLOCK #10—the color's even patented! And there are few more distinctive drivers than Phil Parsons. That's because Phil Parsons is an organizer, an idea man, a leader.

He is, for instance, one of the founders of Motor Racing Outreach and currently serves on the MRO board, along with his wife (and team co–owner), Marcia.

In 1995, he returned to Busch Grand National racing, where he was one of the founding drivers in 1982 after several successful years on the NASCAR Winston Cup side.

But then, Phil comes from a family of winners. He started racing in 1973, the same year his older brother, Benny, won the NASCAR Winston Cup title. And he doesn't show any signs of slowing down. By mid-season 1996, he'd already bettered his fine showing in 1995, finishing third at the Busch Lite 300, the Opryland USA 320, and the Food City 250, then fourth at the Goody's 250, and eighth at the GM Goodwrench/Delco Batteries 200.

I came from a family of believers, but as far as attending church regularly as a family, we didn't. My mom would still dress me up and send me off to church. She always saw to it that I went to church or at least Sunday school anyway.

I think my personal relationship with Jesus came about as a gradual thing. I've always been a believer, but when I met my wife, Marcia, I found that she was a little deeper into the faith. Shortly after that we started attending church regularly. Later still, we got involved with what was the forerunner of Motor Racing Outreach around the NASCAR circuits. So with me it was more of a gradual thing versus being able to say, "Hey, it was August 14, 19–whatever." I've often thought about it in recent years, trying to go back and trace one event, but I just can't. It wouldn't be truthful if I said, "Well, it was this certain day in this certain place" because that really wasn't the case. That's not how God worked with me.

I've just been a believer and prayed all my life, as long as I could remember. Still, I wasn't baptized until 1985 again, mostly through Marcia's efforts.

Is it difficult to maintain your faith? Like most professional athletes, you're working when other people are in church.

I'd say yes. We're fortunate that we're able to have chapel services at the racetracks. We're fortunate that we can still do what we do on Sundays and have church services. Right now I'm running the Busch Grand National Series exclusively, and most of our races are on Saturday. We try to get home and go to our regular church on Sunday in addition to trying to go to the chapel services on the racetracks as much as we can. The Busch Grand National Series chapels are under the auspices of the MRO and Ron and Jackie Pegram are the chaplains there.

Has your experience being an owner and a Christian been different from when you were a racer and a Christian?

Not really. When we hire the people we hire, we don't necessarily try to hire Christians, but we try to be a positive influence on the people we work with. I wouldn't necessarily say that everybody we've hired has been a Christian, but hopefully he or she will be knowledgeable about Christ. As far as being Christians, well, we're working on that!

Memorable Moment

When you do well, it's *always* more memorable! The wins certainly stand out. I'd have to say that my first Busch win back in 1982 was a big moment in my career. That was in Bristol, Tennessee. It's still clear—but then, I can pretty much remember *every* race I've ever run.

Has the taste of victory changed since you've become an owner?

Well, possibly so. We owned our own team from 1991 to 1994 on the Busch Series. One of our major races is at Charlotte, North Carolina, and we won it with our own team with all our own people and friends. That was probably the most gratifying victory or moment we've ever had because it *was* our own team and we were probably underfinanced. But what we lacked in dollars, we made up for in hard work and effort. We were fortunate enough to have a real good car that day, and the breaks went our way, and we won the thing.

DIANNE SIMON

Owner
Dick Simon Racing

Dick Simon was a businessman, driver, and part-time parachutist. Dianne Simon was in real estate. In 1983, they founded a small team. Before (perhaps temporarily) leaving racing in 1996, Dick Simon Racing was a force to be reckoned with at Indy. They've set records for fielding the most teams at the Brickyard on three different occasions. The Simons also became noted as top talent scouts, giving such drivers as Raul Boesel, Arie Luyendyk, Scott Brayton, and Hiro Matsushita early breaks in their careers.

In late 1996, the Simons are currently weighing their options, listening for the still small voice that will tell them whether to reenter Indy Car racing or to enjoy the next set of challenges that God has in store for them elsewhere.

I was raised in a Christian home where we went to church and Sunday school every week. My mother and father attended with us. We only prayed when Grandma visited because she would say the grace on holidays or Sundays when she came to dinner. So it was kind of a mixed message that we got in the home. I left church when I got on my own.

Still, God has been in my life always. When I needed Him, He was always there. He was there before I knew I needed Him on a couple of occasions over my lifetime, but as soon as life turned

■▪■▪■▪■▪■▪■▪■▪■▪■▪■▪■▪■▪■▪■▪■▪■▪■▪■▪■▪■

around, I would just go off down the road and do my own thing and not give Him much thought. But every time I got into trouble, I was back on my knees begging for help.

That changed because of some friends of ours who were Christians. My husband, Dick, and I were successful businesspeople. No matter what business we were in, we were both successful. We'd known these Christian friends, who hadn't always been Christians, for a long time and they were on hard times. We were helping them a little bit here and there, and she bought us a Bible. I knew she couldn't afford that Bible. I had Bibles in the home already, nice Bibles.

The one she gave us was one of those "life application" Bibles. You read the Scripture, then you can read the notes on the text below. It takes Scripture and applies it, asking questions like, "Why is this relevant today? What did this say back then? How can we apply it to our lives today?"

I started reading in the book of John because somewhere along the line somebody told me that's where you should start. I read some more. Then I thought I wanted to read the book of Revelation. So I did. Then I just suddenly had a hunger to read the whole thing. I thought, *I've been starting at the end. I need to start at the beginning.*

I went to the front and I was fascinated by the Old Testament. I started to tell my husband, "This is really important stuff. I think we really need to know more about this. I think we've missed something somewhere."

Reading the Word is what got me totally committed because I've always had a questioning mind. No matter what was said, I questioned it. I thought it was just me—I didn't realize that the things I was questioning had been asked about since the conception of Jesus Himself.

Do you attend any organized fellowship of believers?

Our lifestyle makes it really difficult, and that's why when we were on the circuit, I was glad to have a friend like Hunter Floyd and attend his services there with Motorsports Ministries. Also, it's important to have that community of Christians within the organization because we relate to one another and relate to everything that's going on around us a little bit differently.

It's a real show-biz world in Indy Cars. It's a really "me, me, me" world. Still, it doesn't matter what is happening; I just say, "Excuse me, but I'm going to Chapel right now." If somebody wants to have a team meeting, I ask that they do it some time other than the chapel hour because I want to go to the service. If they want me at their meeting, they will set it some time *other* than during the chapel service. Now, if the schedules run over and I'm out on the line and practice is running through, then I might miss a chapel service, or part of it. But that doesn't happen very often and that isn't something that can be controlled.

I think everybody we work with pretty well just finds out that this is an aspect of our lives, and rather than me imposing it upon anybody, they tend to bring the subject up. Maybe I'm not even consciously aware of the fact that I'm doing that. I don't know—it just seems to always happen. It's a very natural thing.

Dick and I started Dick Simon Racing in 1983. That was our first season as a small team. We did everything. He worked on the race car and drove the race car and sometimes drove the truck. I did all the uniforms and team lunches and all the travel and hotel arrangements. It was a small, mom-and-pop shop. It just grew over the years. It got more sponsorship and more people, and Dick retired from driving in 1988.

From that point on, the team grew really fast because he was concentrating on building it. We hired drivers, and the sponsorship grew because Dick could devote more time to that. All of a sudden, we were running four and five cars at Indianapolis and three cars all season long. Most of that was not because we enjoyed working that hard, but because it took all of that to keep up with the expenses of the circuit. It was so competitive, and everything was obsolete by the next year, so you had to buy all new equipment and things like that. It was kind of like being on a gerbil wheel—just going and going and going and really not getting that much ahead.

We had some success in '93 and '94. We came real close to winning some races, but at the same time, we had a driver and a sponsor whom we had a long-term contract with, and they decided they would be better off if they went to another team. That was a devastating blow—we just could never financially recover from it.

At the end of '95, we actually brought in a partner who ultimately bought us out completely.

Although it was an unfortunate manner in which to have gotten out of racing, all the way through I knew God was in control of everything. I just don't know exactly how He is going to work it all out. Our team was a very close-knit group, and we had a very high number of Christians. All of us were on our knees praying about this situation.

A lot of people on the outside looking in said, "What a crummy, rotten deal. You don't deserve that. You must be so mad." And it *was* disappointing, but when you know God is in control of everything, you wonder how He is going to work it out. Sometimes the not knowing is hardest. You *know* it's going to work out, but in the meantime you're thinking, *Gosh, I don't know whether to take a step with my left foot or my right foot.*

Now that so much time has passed, when I look back I see that it was indeed a lousy, rotten thing that happened to us. But God made sure that everybody got taken care of one way or the other. It wasn't a pleasant situation for anyone. Nevertheless, rather than having to fold up our company and close the door and go bankrupt, the creditors got paid and our employees were kept on. No, they didn't like not working for us, but it kept them employed over the winter months, which is the worst time to be unemployed in the racing industry. Little by little, they've all found their new roads.

Today, everybody is really happy. Everybody is doing different things and we keep in contact. It's like an exciting new adventure.

Memorable Moment

It would have to be in '94 when we almost won the Indy 500. In our sport, the Indy 500 is definitely the big one. We were dominant all month long in May of that year. We were a favorite to win. Our driver, Raul Boesel, qualified on the front row. He wasn't on the pole, but he was on the front row. He took off and led the race right from the green flag. He led the race for a long time and then he made a pit stop and made an infraction on the exit of the pit—he passed Mario Andretti under the yellow. That created a stop-and-go penalty. He had to go all the way to the back. Close to the end of the race, he was all the way back up to fourth when another yellow came out and he was running very strong. If there were enough laps left, he probably would have finished right up there one, two, or three.

On this yellow, the first three cars went around another race car. They passed him under the yellow and he even said, "The first three cars have passed this car. What should I do? Should I go around him too?" We said, "No, you've already been black-flagged once for that. When it goes green, they'll black-flag those three cars and you'll be leading the race. We'll win it."

But they never black-flagged those three guys. It just wasn't one of those things that was meant to be. We ran really strong and everybody knew we were the strongest team there.

I do pray all the time during those situations. I don't pray for a win or anything like that. I always just pray for the best.

NED WICKER

Editor
Indy Car Racing Magazine
Waukesha, Wisconsin

When an Indy Car fan or driver wants to know what's going on in this beloved sport, they reach for a copy of Indy Car Racing Magazine. *Since November 1983,* Indy Car *has been the only magazine devoted exclusively to this fast-paced sport.*

The colorful magazine is published monthly by the husband-and-wife team of Ned and Debbie Wicker and is sold nationwide and throughout Europe and Asia as well. It features solid reporting from the likes of David Phillips and Jeremy Shaw and eye-catching photography from Cheryl Day-Anderson, among others.

But for editor Ned Wicker, it is only the latest tangible example of God's grace and mercy for His people, no matter how undeserving.

My mother was a devout Episcopalian and took me to church. I had somewhat of an interest in it, and I became an acolyte. But I had no idea what I was doing or why I was doing it. So I went to my confirmation classes and I did my acolyte thing. I can remember the day I was confirmed as an Episcopalian because the bishop came. He was a rather impressive man. He laid his hands on my head and said: "You're an Episcopalian."

I said, "I'm a *what?*"

Even in my training as an acolyte, they only taught me how to pour wine. They didn't teach me the ways of the Lord and why I was doing that. I never heard the gospel. It wasn't until much later that I came to any kind of understanding, and it was an odd set of circumstances that brought it about.

I was in an enlisted man's club at a naval base in California. I was a radioman assigned to the U.S.S. *Long Beach,* a beautiful nuclear-powered guided missile cruiser. I was in a club doing my thing, which was trying to hold myself up at the bar while I guzzled beer as fast as it was served.

Meanwhile, a shipmate from my division, Gary Borles, had just been saved. He was on fire for the Lord and he was going to let everyone know it. He saw me inside, walked up to me, and asked me a very simple question, which, at the time, was probably one of the most irritating things I could have heard: "If the Lord Jesus Christ were standing next to you right now, would you be getting drunk?"

Gary didn't say anything else, he just wanted to ask me that question.

That irritated me so much that the following day, when I was sober again, I went up to Gary and asked, "What were you up to?" And he told me. But nothing sank in. I thought, *Oh brother, what do we have here? What's going on? Just two weeks ago Gary and I were partying hard together. Now this.*

At the same time, there was another radioman, Larry Taylor from Texas. Larry was ten years older than me—I was only about twenty then—and he'd gone to a Bible college in Springfield, Missouri. He'd been trained for the ministry, or at least he'd gone through their pastoral program. Larry was a much more mature Christian, and he had been working with Gary. While Gary was on fire and out there to really make his mark, Larry took his time and was much calmer. It was Larry who really started to explain to me the things of the Lord, what it means to have a personal relationship with Jesus Christ.

In time, they invited me to go to church with them. It was a Baptist church in town just off base. I can't remember the name of it, but Gary was in the choir. In fact, I do not recall the service at all. The only lasting impression that I had was during the altar call while the choir was singing. Gary came down out of the choir to where I was sitting and said, "Can you not feel it? Isn't this getting to you? Don't you understand?"

I looked at him a long time. I said, "Gary, it looks like everybody is having a real good time, but I'm afraid I'm just not with you here. I don't understand." Gary was a little put off by that.

Later, Larry gave me a tract titled "The Roman Road to Salvation." It was a simple little Bible tract, but after reading it, I started to understand the concept of sin, the reason God created us, and how the sin in your life will separate you from God. Before that, I'd always thought, *I'm a good guy. I've never done anything bad to anybody. I have a couple of vices, but other than that, there's nothing too wrong with me.* But from "The Roman Road," I learned that "*All* have sinned and fall short of the glory of God" (Rom. 3:23). I pondered that for a moment. What did that mean?

Then I read the statement, "The wages of sin is death" (Rom. 6:23). What do they mean, the *wages* of sin is death? What sin?

But the more I read, the more nervous I got. I started thinking, *Man, maybe I've got something to think about here.* This went on for a few months.

Finally, aboard the ship, on either the twentieth or twenty-first of September in 1971, I couldn't stand it anymore. I was walking around with this brick on my head. I didn't know how or what or why: *Why am I upset? Why am I carrying this around with me?* I met with Larry and said, "I've got to get rid of this."

We were in the berthing compartment—forty-seven guys lived in a space that was thirty feet by thirty feet, stacked three high—but he and I knelt down and Larry said, "You've got to go to the Lord with this."

I pretty much understood that the way to reach the Lord was through the Lord Jesus Christ. I said, "I want to be my Father's son here." Larry led me to the Lord that day.

I had a basic, cursory understanding of what it meant to be in communion with the Lord. But for the first time, I felt really good about it. In that instant, that load was lifted off of my shoulders and all of the little things that were festering inside of me were gone.

I feel the same way now about being saved as when I *was* saved. It just astonishes me! I'm nothing, I'm nobody! And the

Lord loves me. He's shown me His grace and His goodness, and I don't understand. I just marvel in it.

God created us with free will, and that makes it all the more marvelous. We come to Him because we want to, we need to. For some of us who are a little hardheaded, maybe it just takes longer than others.

I got into racing by accident. In 1979, a friend called and said that her mother worked for the promoter at the Milwaukee Mile. The company she worked for also owned *The Midwest Racing News*, and they needed somebody part-time to help them with writing. I was working for the Associated Press at the time, covering baseball, occasionally football and college basketball, even the Milwaukee Bucks on occasion. I was looking for some extra money, so when this position opened up, I went over to the office and said, "I can give you a few hours a week. Here's my baseball schedule. As long as it doesn't interfere, it's fine." They hired me.

But once I worked in racing, I got the bug in a hurry. Through Hale's Corners, which ran late-model stock cars, along with occasional Midgets and sprint cars, and through my working with *The Midwest Racing News* and writing about virtually *all* forms of auto racing, I got hooked.

In 1983, I went to work for Miller Brewing Company doing public relations for Al Unser, the defending national champion at the time. I also worked for Vandervell, an engine-bearing manufacturer and the sponsor of the Rookie of the Year program in Indy Car racing. I was full-time on the Indy Car circuit from 1984 to 1986. I also worked for Hemelgarn Racing, the team that won the Indy 500 in 1996.

In 1987 I was helping out at the St. Petersburg Grand Prix with a friend of mine, Jan Shaffer, the public relations director at Michigan International Speedway and the Championship Auto Racing Team (CART). Jan was having a discussion with a motorsports photographer named Steve Snoddy. He and Steve were discussing Rob Griggs, of Griggs Publishing Company, in Concord, North Carolina. Rob wanted to sell *Indy Car Racing Magazine*, which really wasn't succeeding. It had become a tabloid newspaper that came out every two weeks.

I said, "Could I play? I could add a shekel or two to the deal.

I have a Macintosh computer and I might even be able to help you out on the production of this thing." This is all pre-desktop publishing, remember—I had no idea what I was talking about. But I did know that I was interested.

So we all decided that we were going to get together and make Griggs an offer. We did, he agreed, and the three of us became the owners of *Indy Car Racing Magazine*—grossly undercapitalized, flying by the seat of our pants, and knowing nothing of what we were supposed to be doing.

Steve later decided he wanted to remain as a photographer, but he wasn't in a position to be an owner of the magazine. Steve sold his share to Jan and remained as our photographer.

I did all of the production side; Jan coordinated most of the writing. I don't know how it worked, but it did. We put out our first edition in April 1988—there was a month lag between Griggs's last edition and our first.

It was ghastly. Terrible. I did a lousy production job. The writing was very good, though. Jan, who now does public relations for the Indy Racing League, is an exceptional writer. I just loved having him as my partner because he really taught me a lot about magazine writing.

We operated as a tabloid newspaper for a couple of years. But it was always in the back of my mind to bring the magazine back to where it started as a glossy publication. The first step in 1990 was to put it back into a magazine form. We did. It was still all on newsprint, but at least it was in magazine format.

Jan came to me one day and said, "Ned, I believe that *Indy Car Racing Magazine* can support one guy, but I don't believe it can support two. Would you like to buy me out?" By 1990, I had it on my own—I was editor *and* publisher. I came in as advertising manager, then managing editor, then I was running the whole show with another individual.

And it was going nowhere. We were flailing away. After being a pulp magazine, it now had a slick cover on it with a nice color photograph. We operated that way for a while. We were publishing after every race because every race is a big event. I had this crazy notion that we could succeed that way. And we lost money hand over fist.

While all of this was going on, my wife, Debbie, was an associate partner with Anderson Consulting. Debbie is an exceptional computer systems designer. Her specialty was building mechanized billing systems for huge public utilities. She devised a product at Anderson Consulting called "Customer One" and turned this into this huge enterprise within Anderson Consulting. She had fifty-two people working on the project with her. And, God love her, she left it all to help me save *Indy Car Racing*.

Now here's the wonderful part, the part where it all ties together: About six months or so after I was saved, I had gone my own way. But God said, "That's okay, Ned, go ahead. I'm here." Now we're at 1991. *Twenty years of doing nothing!* But God stuck with me the whole time, whether I knew it or not.

So we were at Indianapolis in 1991 and I was on the phone with Debbie. We were losing money, we had problems with an employee, and I was in huge trouble. In the midst of all of that, the Holy Spirit tapped me on the shoulder and said, "Are you ready yet?"

I threw my hands up in the air and said, "Lord, I'm done. I can't do this. I'm stupid. I'm really, really dumb. Help me."

I went to Hunter Floyd. I said, "Hunter, I can't do this. I've got an employee I want to kill. I've not been walking with the Lord. Help me get back on track!" I found myself in the Tower Terrace, watching practice and praying with Hunter.

I wasn't praying for God to save my business. I was praying for God to help me do what I was supposed to do. "Dear God, help me conduct business the right way. Help me deal with this employee in the way You would deal with him. Please give me wisdom, Lord. Just push me, and I'll go anywhere You want me to go. I give up." Then I went back to work.

After a lot of prodding and gentle cajoling, the employee still wouldn't come clean. We let him go.

Then the printer came up and said, "You know, you're really behind. I don't think I want to print your magazine anymore."

That's when Debbie got involved. She said to the printer, "I'll give you a deal. You have a chance of maybe recouping your money if you print one more issue for us. If you don't, we'll go out of business and you'll get nothing."

The printer thought about it and said, "Okay."

Then we changed to monthly. After the Portland race in 1991, we put in a couple of features and said, "This is the July issue and

▪◻▪◻▪◻▪◻▪◻▪◻▪◻▪◻▪◻▪◻▪◻▪◻▪◻▪◻▪◻▪◻▪◻▪◻▪◻

you'll get another issue in August. We're going monthly from now on!" That meant we didn't have to print anything until the end of July, which gave us time to hustle up and start getting things together.

The Lord said, "Okay, Ned. You're $75,000 to $100,000 in the hole. I'm going to help you." And He did. The response to *Indy Car Racing Magazine* going monthly was very positive. Advertisers liked it, subscribers liked it, everyone liked it. It was a hit. I didn't think it looked like much, but instead of being on newsprint, we were now on slick paper, and we published some color pictures here and there inside—mostly black and white, but still, it was an improvement.

With the Lord's help, we dug in and began doing our thing and working as hard as we could. The whole time, I kept saying to the Lord, "I want to walk with You. If You want to trash the magazine, go ahead. It's okay. I just want to be with You."

With Debbie's brilliant organizational and computer skills and the Lord's help, things began to happen. All of a sudden, Debbie discovered that, as a publisher, we were tax-exempt on printing! It was the law. We went to the printer and said, "Look, we owe you forty thousand dollars, but for two or three years here you've been charging us sales tax."

He said, "You know, you're right." So there was a savings of ten thousand dollars right there.

There was a loan I had gotten from a friend to help keep the magazine afloat. Suddenly, that was forgiven. Thirty thousand dollars! Then a couple of advertisers said, "Yeah, we'll help you out." By the end of the year, by at least November, we'd gone from owing $75,000 to $100,000 in June—"We're toast"—to being flush! I was astounded. The Lord made it happen.

When something really neat happens, you know how you're kind of giddy? That's how I felt then. I still feel that way.

I don't deserve the Lord's grace—I just get it. It astonishes me every day.

SCOTT SHARP

Driver
#1
Indy Racing League
Conseco/A. J. Foyt Dallara/Oldsmobile

There was never much doubt Scott Sharp would eventually win an Indy Racing League event. After all, he'd won big in every division he'd competed in during his short career. Still, it came as a surprise to some that he won the True Value 200 in Loudon, New Hampshire, on August 18, 1996, so decisively in just his second full year of Indy-style racing. And, perhaps more impressively, Scott was one of the IRL's point leaders by mid-season.

There is, of course, the matter of bloodlines to consider. Scott is the son of six-time national SCCA champion Bob Sharp. He drives for racing legend A. J. Foyt. And his wife, Kim, is the daughter of Trans Am veteran Greg Pickett.

Still, there is the strong possibility of talent at work here. Scott won three straight SCCA national titles and two straight GT-1 titles in the 1980s, including the SCCA National GT-2 Driver's Championship in a Nissan 280ZX Turbo for Newman-Sharp Racing—headed by his father and Paul Newman (yes, that Paul Newman) in 1986.

Then in 1991 he won six races en route to the Trans Am Championship, setting seven track records along the way. In 1993, Scott made his debut in PPG Cup racing and won his second Trans Am title in three years. He qualified for Indy the following year and ran all sixteen PPG Cup races with a best finish of ninth at Phoenix.

Scott was named A. J. Foyt's driver for the 1995 Indy and both have prospered ever since from the partnership. And at that point, it was indeed just a matter of time.

I was fortunate enough to be brought up in a real Christian family. From an early age, my mom made sure God was a high priority in my life. I started going to church when I was very young, and I've carried that through my whole life. My decision to follow Jesus happened when I was pretty young. Since then, in the racing world—and in all of life—there are continual reminders occurring, telling you exactly where your faith needs to be.

What's really great for me is Motorsports Ministries and their contribution to motor racing. They have a couple of different services, generally every Sunday morning. The services provide a good hour of quality time to help you stay focused and remind yourself what it is all about.

Unfortunately, motor racing is a very roller-coaster type of career, and there are many more lows than highs. I think having a strong faith in God helps keep you centered in *all* of those lows and those highs. It keeps you focused on why you're really there and what your job is. And maybe it isn't always driving a race car—there is a greater picture, after all.

It seems there are more and more drivers who are starting to attend the Motorsports Ministries services. It's great to see them slowly coming over. As a driver, you never know—any minute might be your last. You have to be prepared for that in any time of life, even walking across the road to get your mail, for that matter. But I think more drivers are Christians than people realize, than I know, but many of them may be more private in their beliefs.

Certainly in 1996, Indy Car had its fair share of tragic losses. I wonder sometimes how people who don't have a strong religious faith can deal with it and have their many questions answered. Perhaps that's one of the reasons more and more people are attending the services. It's great that Motorsports Ministries is at the races and provides more than just services—it provides counseling, Bible studies, consultation, prayer meetings, whatever is needed.

Memorable Moment

Certainly winning my first Indy Car race on August 18 in Loudon, New Hampshire, has been the most memorable moment of my career thus far. It was something I'd worked long and hard for. I was so happy to be able to bring the trophy home for the team and my team owner, A. J. Foyt.

As we neared the checkered flag, lots of thoughts were running through my head, but the main one was of appreciation. I was very thankful for the opportunity, thankful for the trust, hoping there would be a way I could use this success to further God's reach in some way.

That final lap, interestingly enough, is an incredibly tedious period. You think you'd be at the ultimate high, but you really aren't until you finally cross that checkered flag. I think you become ten times as sensitive to the little nuances of the car, exactly where you are and what's going on. You become overly critical of anything that might tamper with the victory.

And there at the Winner's Circle, certainly it's a time to be very jovial and it's hard to suppress the excitement. At the same time, I distanced myself a little and realized my main emotion was one of gratitude. I felt at that moment that it was so rewarding, and I felt like I needed to use it in some form to extend myself—more than just standing up there, shaking hands and spraying champagne—to really stretch and give back a little bit in terms of my faith and in terms of my sport. To give something back in every way.

Norm Miller

Sponsor
Chairman of the Board, Interstate Batteries
#18
Joe Gibbs Racing
Interstate Batteries Monte Carlo

The best thing you can say about somebody these days is, "He walks his talk."

That's what they say about Norm Miller.

Even nonracing fans know that he's the chairman of the $350 million per year Interstate Batteries System of America, Inc.—the world's number-one-selling brand of replacement batteries with 330 distributors and 200,000 dealers in North America. What they may not know is that he commits $3 million per year to ensure that the film Jesus is distributed around the world to believers and unbelievers alike.

And when Norm got involved with NASCAR, he did it with his integrity, financial acumen, and strong faith intact. Today, the Interstate Batteries/Joe Gibbs Racing team is a prime example of what's right about the sport, noted both for its excellence and its top-to-bottom Christian commitment.

My father was an alcoholic during the first eight years of my life. After he quit drinking, we went to church and I won awards for attending so many Sundays and memorizing verses, but I never had any recollection of it being personal or going deeper than just thought. My father became a deacon at the First Christian Church we attended in Galveston, Texas.

Galveston was a big party town. Most everything that went on there was illegal back when I was growing up. There were gambling, liquor by the drink, and open prostitution twenty-four hours a day. As a young guy at age fourteen, I started drinking and lived this lifestyle. My whole goal in life was to have fun. About that time I quit going to church. Nobody made me go. I forgot about church till I was about thirty-five years old. At that stage, things happened. One was that I had set a bunch of goals for myself when I was getting ready to get out of college and I had achieved them all ahead of time. They weren't real big, but they were mine. So I experienced an emptiness; I wondered what was wrong. I thought reaching my goals would make me happy. Those things are supposed to do that.

The second thing was that I realized I had become an alcoholic just like my father. At that juncture, real desperation hit me one morning and I blurted out, "God, help me. I can't handle it." This from a guy who had started drinking when he was fourteen and had continued drinking steadily for twenty years and had even experienced blackouts. My whole social life involved drinking. After my prayer, God took this compulsion away, so I knew something had happened.

At the same time, within a couple of weeks, a friend named Tom Crocker began to tell me that the Bible was the Word of God, intended to tell you how to live life. I questioned him and told him I thought it was an old book by a bunch of old guys from a long time ago. He told me it was the Word of *God*. So I said, "Prove it."

I thought I'd run him off, but Tom got some materials and books by Josh McDowell and the ancient writings of Josephus and some archaeological things for me. I did a study on whether there was any basis to believe the Bible or not. I was overwhelmed with the evidence. After looking at all the data, I realized that the Bible was truth.

From that, I began to read the Bible and go to a Bible study. I began to see how it applied to my life and saw that God was a good and loving God—but that I had a problem with my sins. At age thirty-five I prayed one night to receive Christ. I asked Him to forgive me and put His Spirit in my heart and help me live a life that would please Him. I was discipled by Search Ministries, an evangelistic discipleship ministry that works with professional golfers.

Have you had opportunities to share your faith in NASCAR?

I gave a brief testimony when we first got started in motor racing in 1992 at the Daytona 500, where Joe Gibbs and I sponsored a dinner for all the NASCAR family. This was our entrance into a full season of racing with Joe Gibbs and vice versa for him. We wanted to do an outreach, so we had a dinner that night and I gave a short testimony there.

Since then, we've made some tracts, but they feature more about Joe and Interstate Batteries. I'm not in those tracts personally, but Interstate is. We have tracts that we pass out with the show cars at different events, and I've given my testimony there at the chapel services.

I pray regularly for our driver, Bobby Labonte, our team, and their families. I also pray for Dale Jarrett—he was our driver before Bobby—and his wife, Kelley, and their kids and family. I also pray every race for God's blessing and safety and ask for help for everybody. When we pray before the race, we also pray for the people in the stands coming and going.

Memorable Moment

I have two, actually. One would be when we won Daytona in 1993. That was just a complete shock to me, though I know the team knew we had a really good car. It was our second Daytona. As far as the Joe Gibbs Racing team, it was our thirty-second race and to go out and win Daytona was just phenomenal.

When you're so new, you don't really know what's happening. I enjoyed Daytona, but I didn't understand what a tremendous accomplishment it was for all the participants, for the team, and for Jimmy Makar and Dale Jarrett, because we just hadn't been around for that long.

But last year, when we won Michigan with Bobby

Labonte—especially when you know how hot Jeff Gordon was last year to win the points championship—that was just as special. We'd been in the lead and when Jeff passed Bobby with about ten laps to go, I thought, *Oh, no, not this Gordon thing again.* We'd already finished second twice to him in 1995. I love Jeff Gordon, but you want your team to win.

Then Bobby passed him with about six laps left, and I thought that was something extra! To be in the lead and have Gordon pass us near the finish there and for Bobby to pass him again and hold on and win, now *that* was a great victory!

Do you pray during the races as well as before them?

We thank God. I forget sometimes, but I try to remember to thank Him at the end of every race no matter what happens. I know that God knows best and whatever happens there He's promised He'll work it for good for those of us who love Him and are called according to His purpose. I certainly don't want to get in the middle of it! So we just pray to do our best and tell Him that if He lets us win, we'll honor Him. We go with that and don't look back.

We try to go with the attitude of "Alleluia!" no matter what happens. We know that He is a good and loving God with kind intentions and loves us beyond what we can even conceive, so that whatever comes from His hand is good. And that's the way I try to look at it.

Troy Selberg

Crew Chief
#75
Butch Mock Motorsports/Remington Racing
Ford Thunderbird

When the beautiful kelly/forest (don't ever say green in racing) and gold Remington Arms #75 roars out of the pit, look for Troy Selberg, one of the best young crew chiefs in the nation watching it go. Nineteen ninety-six marked Troy's third year with Mock Motorsports, though he's already worked with the likes of Ricky Rudd, Darrell Waltrip, and Lake Speed in his short career.

For Troy, part of the attraction of working with Mock has been the opportunity to be crew chief for driver Morgan Shepherd, one of racing's sturdiest and most respected veterans. And for Shepherd (now approaching his thirtieth year in the sport and well over $6 million in NASCAR Winston Cup earnings) to place his complete faith in the fresh-faced young man from a small town in California, is high praise indeed.

I grew up in a racing family in Porterville, California. My dad drove race cars. After he was in a wreck, my mother decided that he didn't need to drive anymore. My dad continued to drive for a while after that but eventually left it and just worked on the cars.

Well, all my dad's friends, some of whom now own Winston

Cup teams, moved out to North Carolina in 1967 because it had become the hotbed of NASCAR racing. One day Dad came home and said, "Guess what! We're moving to North Carolina." He owned two service stations and had his little race shop, but we packed everything up and moved to a small town called Mount Pleasant, which is right outside of Concord, North Carolina.

My dad went to work for D. K. Ulrich. D. K. had been in the business for some time and was from the same town that we were. There are about seven or eight mechanics on the circuit today that are all from this same small hometown, and they all raced this race-track called Bakersfield, which is now Mason Moran Raceway.

On the weekends I would go to the races and work on the race car or sweep the pits and do all the things that kids would do. I liked it.

We moved again in the middle of the school year, which was kind of tough on me. We'd been there about a year and I had established some friends in Mount Pleasant. So when my parents moved to Charlotte, I didn't want to go. My best friend's father was a minister. His family said, "Why don't you let Troy stay with us, and he can finish out the school year here? After school's out in the summer he can move to Charlotte."

That was really the turning point. The seed was sown but I didn't reap right then. At my new home, we would say a prayer before a meal, which was new to me. Along the way I asked a few questions here and there, but I was still kind of timid about it.

I was in a car accident in 1985. I remember it vividly, like it was yesterday. I hit a tree. It knocked the windshield out and I could reach out and touch the tree. I was pinned in the car. When they came to get me, they said, "Don't move and we'll get you out." I remember them taking the seat and the rear window out, and then I blacked out.

The next thing I remember, I'm riding down the road and I'm thinking, *This thing has got the awfulest shocks on it in the whole world.* I knew I was in an ambulance. The paramedics were saying, "Come on, man, you can make it."

I thought, *Who in the world are they talking about? Oh, they're talking about me!* I said, "Hey, I'm fine."

They shouted, "He's coming around!"

I thought, *What do you mean, "coming around"? I'm fine.* I found out later I almost died.

At the hospital, they found I had ruptured my spleen, broken my hip and my leg, and cut my face up pretty good. I was in traction for a month in the hospital.

And that's when I started studying the Bible. I was pretty shaken up by how close I came to dying and I gave myself to the Lord. But with no follow-up, nothing happened. Still, I had learned a little bit when I was staying at my friend's house, and I learned a little bit more in the hospital.

When I got out, I met my wife. She has a Christian background. When she asked me about my faith, I said, "Oh, yeah, I gave my life to the Lord when I was in the hospital."

Then she goes, "Good. Then we've got to find a church before we get married."

We started looking around and finally found a church. It took about three months of going to church in the off-season for me to figure out, *Yeah, I know who this Guy is. But you know, I need to give my life to the Lord publicly.* So one Sunday in church I stood up and said, "I'm going down there and giving my life to the Lord." And my wife-to-be started going crazy, crying and all that stuff.

It's still new to me. And it's been a growing process ever since because in the business that we're in, we don't have Sunday. It's not like, "We're going to Sunday school and we're going to learn some things. And then we're going to listen to the minister on Sunday at 11:00." In racing, the only way you can learn and grow is by reading the Bible and trying to interpret it yourself, which is pretty tough to do, or by having someone like Bob Dyar go to lunch with you every Monday. Bob's been a real inspiration. People like Bob and Max Helton can show you the way through.

Memorable Moment

I've been in Victory Lane several times. Probably the one that stands out the most is so special because we didn't have any money; that was with Lake Speed in 1993. It was Lake Speed Racing, and Purex was the sponsor. It was the Dial-Purex Ford Thunderbird, car #83.

We had shown up at the Coca-Cola 600. And when I tell you we showed up with no money, I'll tell you the actual figures, because it's astounding. We originally ran twelve races on $300,000! And we did it with guys who had never been in Winston Cup racing before.

Lake originally said, "I want to form a Christian race team." But I said, "Lake, you're not going to be able to do that. The Lord's going to send us people for a reason, and they might not be Christians when they come down this driveway. And He might send them down this driveway for you, not for them." He understood that.

We brought these people in and showed them how to do it correctly. We taught them how to change tires and to jack the car up right. A couple years later, many of these guys have come back and said, "You guys have been so inspirational in getting me to where I am." We had one kid, eighteen years old, who couldn't walk and chew bubble gum at the same time. Today, he's one of the best tire changers on the Winston Cup circuit.

So we're at the Coca-Cola 600 and we're running third. We've run fast the whole time we're there. We come in, make a pit stop, and go up to second. The crowd is just having a fit because we beat Dale Earnhardt out of the pits and they're going, "How about this car?!"

After we've done that two or three times, people are saying, "These guys are a real threat to win today!"

Unfortunately, the last time we came down pit road, because we didn't have a lot of money, we had some equipment that wasn't up to par. We were making a pit stop under a caution when we stopped and changed the tires. But when Lake went to take off, a gear broke. We were going to beat them that day because *we were right there.*

We pushed her back in and fixed it and went back on the racetrack. We ran good the rest of the day, but we were *that* close. We finished about seventeenth or nineteenth. Of course, the record books don't say, "Finished eighteenth but could have won the race."

Fortunately, everybody in the garage area sees that, and they still talk about it today. People will tell me, "That car—you had that race won."

Sometimes you go to Victory Lane and you *knew* you were going to go there anyway. You had the best team and the best money—so big deal. It's those other times that I remember best.

DALE JARRETT

Driver
#88
Ford Quality Care
Robert Yates Racing Ford Thunderbird

Nineteen ninety-six was the breakthrough year for Dale Jarrett. Sure, he'd won a total of four races in the past (including the 1993 Daytona 500), but nothing could compare with 1996, when he won four major races—including another Daytona 500 and the second Brickyard 400 at Indianapolis—he finished third in the Winston Cup standings with more than $2 million in total winnings.

Perhaps it was the car. Owner Robert Yates purchased his old #88, a number that zoomed across the finish line a host of times when Yates was head engine builder for DiGard Racing. Perhaps it was the advice of his father, Ned, himself a winner of fifty NASCAR races and the voice of CBS Sports's coverage of both his son's Daytona 500 victories. Perhaps it was the muscular red, white, and blue Thunderbird, lovingly crafted by crew chief Todd Parrott and his crack team. Or perhaps it was the support of his wife, Kelley, and their four kids, ranging in ages from two to twenty-one.

Perhaps it was all of the above.

"God has really blessed me," Dale says shyly. "I know I'm very fortunate to have the people surrounding me that I do. Jesus is certainly the reason I have anything that I have."

It's good to be on the winning team.

I was brought up in church, believing in God from as far back as I can remember. My parents, Ned and Martha Jarrett, instilled in each of us Christian values. Of course, with my situation as it is now, our church attendance is limited more to the off–season. But we certainly are a part of a church now. We were and still are a Christian family. This is how we live our lives. These are the rules that we go by.

As a teenager and young adult, I didn't look to God when I was searching for answers to things. I tried to answer them myself more. So I grew apart in my faith a little bit. It wasn't that I ever lost my faith in God, it was just that I didn't call on Him or live my life totally under His rules.

But as I grew older and thought things were more in Dale Jarrett's hands, I began to live my life more under His influence. It was actually about as recently as late 1991, early 1992, that things changed. There was a specific event—the beginning of my association with Joe Gibbs, when he first came to Kelley and me, asking me to drive for the race team he was starting. I already knew a lot about Joe Gibbs, but it was in that time of negotiations that I came to know Joe Gibbs the Christian.

We were actually at the 1992 chapel service for the players for the Super Bowl, which was in Minneapolis, when we rededicated our lives to Christ. It just seemed to be an appropriate time. Kelley and I were very moved by everything that took place, and the speaker was fantastic that night. Certainly Joe was a big part of the reason that we decided this was the time and the place for us to get our lives back in order.

It is from that time forward that I've had a peace of mind and an understanding that we as a family need to live our lives under the rules of God, and we have become much better Christians. Certainly we have times when we fail. But we try to limit those and bring our three kids up in a Christian home and involve them in our church here and in MRO as much as we can.

Memorable Moment

Certainly my successes in racing stand out in my mind. But that one particular night in Minnesota stands out in my mind more than anything else.

As far as on the racetrack, it would be hard to single one out. My first victory in 1991 at Michigan certainly stands out. The Daytona 500 in 1993 with Joe Gibbs and Jimmy Makar was just a tremendous feeling—just to see Joe Gibbs's face was special. I mean, this was a man who had achieved tremendous success in another profession, and to see his face and his actions that day was almost beyond words.

Then in 1996, the whole year has kind of been a dream! We won the Daytona 500 again, the Coca-Cola 600, the Brickyard 400, and the GM Goodwrench Dealer 400 all in one year. It was incredible.

Each and every victory has a special meaning within itself because each one is so different. I can still pretty much go back and describe each and every lap, especially the victories, recalling the specific details in events that took place and how everything evolved.

LANNY BARNES

Engine R&D
#42
Team SABCO
Coors Light Racing Pontiac

By day (and into most nights), soft-spoken Lanny Barnes is the engineer assembler for Team SABCO. He also assembles all of the supertruck engines for Joe Sauter and the #42 supertruck. Lanny's been with Felix Sabates's team for years, through thick and thin. And in the evenings, he may walk around the now-quiet construction site next door with driver Kyle Petty, inspecting SABCO's ambitious expansion campaign.

Whatever he's doing, Lanny Barnes is the consummate team player. During his so-called lunch break you may find him busy assisting chief engine builder David Evans or tinkering with the Pontiac Gran Prix Coupe's 830-cfm, four-barrel induction system. In short, he'll do whatever's needed for Team SABCO's Winston Cup cars.

"We all work together as a unit in the engine shop," Lanny says modestly.

The proof is in the rock-solid craftsmanship of every brick red, yellow, and black #42.

My family was involved in church when I was a child. We grew up in a Methodist church in

Gastonia, South Carolina. As far back as I can remember, we only had one service a week—Sunday morning. So that was the thing to do.

As a youth, I was sprinkled in the church and baptized in the Father, Son, and Holy Ghost. But when I got to be about twelve or thirteen, we quit going to church. Like a lot of young people, I kind of drifted away from church after that.

Still, the Bible promises that if you'll raise your children in the way they should go, they'll come back when they're older. That's exactly what happened to me. As I got older, I was searching for something but I really didn't know what it was. I got into racing before I even got out of high school and at sixteen or seventeen years old I was traveling all over the country with Morgan Shepherd. He was a newly reborn Christian at the time and a great influence on me.

Meanwhile, I couldn't find a lady. I couldn't find a woman that I really wanted to settle down with. I was having some real trouble in that area. One night, I went out with some friends but I was real unhappy. I was about as lonely as a man could be. I finally came home that night, got down beside my bed, and I said to the Lord, "I'm twenty-three already. Please send me a wife. Please send me someone who will follow Your message."

It wasn't long after that that Morgan suggested I meet a young lady named Staci who lived near him in Hickory, North Carolina. I got to know her and a year and a half later, we got married! Today we have two kids and we still live near Morgan.

When I met my wife, everything changed. She's been more than just a wife to me. It is a special marriage—I believe she was sent from God. I was pretty much out of church between the ages of fourteen and twenty-two. Throughout that period, I was searching, trying to find a church home. Now we go to Word of Truth Assembly in Newton, North Carolina, a nondenominational church. Our pastor, Glenn Miller, has become like a second father to us. We have our blood kin, but then we have our church home as well. It's good.

Memorable Moment

I think it was our first Rockingham win in 1990. We led 462 of a possible 489 laps. We sat on the pole, led the most laps, won the race, and collected something like $298,000! It was the largest payday in NASCAR history at the time.

As that last lap neared an end, I remember saying, "Thank You, Lord," over and over because I wanted to give Him credit for everything.

And we were a team. At that time, there were only twelve members on our race team and we were like a family. We were together as a race team *more* than with our families at home. You go to lunch together and, when you're out on the road together, you eat dinner every night together. There's a sense of togetherness, of oneness. You've got to think as one to be a winning team.

That's the difference between our team and others. A lot of teams are comprised of individuals. Those teams may have some success, but not a lot. But the teams that work together with one another for one common goal, they're the ones that win.

When I was younger, I just always thought, *I've got to be at the top, I've got to be at the top. I want to be the man, I want to be the crew chief.* But as you grow older as a Christian, you don't necessarily have to be on top. I've seen that, a lot of times, the Lord can use you better when you're not.

JON BEEKHUIS

Television Motor-Racing Announcer

At the age of six, Jon Beekhuis attended a little driver's school for Quarter-Midget racers. After the school, a family friend asked, "Little boy, what do you want to be when you grow up?" Without hesitation, he replied "I'm going to be a race car driver."

The adult, thinking this racing fixation was just a passing fancy, said, "When you're finished being a race car driver, what would you like to be after that?"

Jon said, "I'm going to make a movie."

Jon was right on nearly all counts. He cut short a promising career in Indy-style racing to become one of television's top commentators.

Equally impressive has been Jon's growth as a Christian. He's only been a believer for a few years, but today Jon and his wife, Jennifer, host a Bible study and work closely with Hunter Floyd in Motorsports Ministries.

Although I came from a family with a Lutheran background, most of my early years were not spent going to church. They were spent in cars. Six years old, believe it or not, was my age when I drove my first race car. At twelve, I won five out of my first six races. They knocked me out of the novice class because I was too fast for the novices, and I went on to be the fastest qualifier for the western states championships in Quarter-Midgets. I absolutely loved it, and that's what I lived for.

I bought a street car at about fifteen, and then I spent some time with my dad. Being an engineer, he showed me all the ins and outs of working on cars and how to prepare them. But because I was so focused on trying to figure out how to be a professional driver, I wasn't spending very much time on school, and my parents—and especially my grandparents—were very concerned because I wasn't getting very good grades. They made me a deal: "Jon, if you can get through high school with a certain grade point average, we will send you to a race car driver school in Canada when you turn eighteen."

That was just the carrot I needed. All of a sudden, I buckled down and I worked hard and all I thought about day and night was getting a chance to go to the Jim Russell Racing School in Montreal. We chose that because I was told by someone it was the best school that you could go to in the world. I pushed and pushed and when my high school graduation came around, I was successful.

At the Jim Russell School in Montreal, I was chosen as the best student in my class. I won the Jim Russell North America Scholarship competition and eventually won their World Scholarship competition, which gave me a scholarship to start racing in England in Formula 4 and get started in my career. That was a dream come true because I didn't have any other way to raise money or to start with sponsorship at a professional level. I raced in England for three years. I did two years of Formula 4 and a year of Formula 3, both of which were quite successful. Then I ran into sponsorship troubles and came back to the U.S. I didn't have any money to continue racing, so I worked on crews of race cars just hoping for an opportunity to get to drive one of them. I drove in various series: Super V, Formula 4, even the IMSA Series. I was just trying to scrounge up a "ride," as we call it.

Finally, I got six investors, and we all put in the same amount of money and traveled around together. With them I went on to win the 1986 Russell Pro Series Championship. That was my first major championship, and it really set the wheels in motion.

After that, I expanded this same group of investors to a bigger group. In 1987, I did the Formula Atlantic Series. In 1988, I did what was then called the American Racing Series, which is now called Indy Lights. I won that championship too, so I'd won two championships in two years.

The prize for winning the Indy Lights Championship was to get a test in an Indy Car. I tested with Tony Bettenhausen's Indy Car team. It was very successful and the following year, 1989, he asked me to come drive for them in Toronto for my Indy Car debut. We had a good race. I had some mechanical problems, so I think we finished sixteenth. But that was the birth of my Indy Car career.

Then I joined a team called PIG Enterprises. The guy who owned the team was Norm Turley, a Long Beach police officer. PIG racing progressed to the point where they ran the Russell Pro Series with me and we won it. Then when I went up a class, so did they. They then went to Atlantic cars. The following year I had an offer to drive for somebody else who was going to foot the bill, so I went with them. But I returned to PIG Racing in '88, and that's when we won the Indy Lights Championship.

In '90, I went back to PIG as they made their jump to Indy Car racing as I did. We did nearly a full season. We had a year-old car, and we didn't have the proper equipment to make a run at the front. But we would generally qualify in the top fifteen. For us, if we qualified eleventh or twelfth out of a field of thirty with a year-old car, we were heroes. I believe my best finish that year was eighth at the Michigan 500.

During all of this, a firm in Indianapolis asked me if I would like to do a little television commentary for the Indy Light Series because I had just won the championship the year before. They needed somebody to sub for only one or two races as the analyst for Indy Light. That was my start in television. So I got a start in Indy Car racing and a start in television both in 1989.

I had a pretty good year going in 1990. I was living a dream. I was absolutely on top of the world. But something happened in about the middle of the season. When the races were over, I would wake up on Monday morning and it was obvious to me that something was not right in my life. I didn't know exactly what it was. I just wondered, since I was finally getting to do what I always wanted to do, why I didn't feel better the next day. There was a big void when I would get home from the racetrack or have any quiet time to myself.

One day, I overheard a fan say, "That Jon Beekhuis, he can really drive a race car, but he is a jerk." I didn't understand why this person had said that, and it really bothered me. I started to try to find out why.

The only thing important to me from age six to age thirty was that I did whatever it took to make me go faster in a race car. I would not even turn on the television or eat a meal without first asking myself, "Is this going to make me go any faster in a race car, and if it's not, is there something that would better my chances—like going to the gym or training or reading technical manuals—I should do instead?"

I even banned my family from the racetrack because I thought they affected my concentration. If I had girlfriends whom I thought were affecting my concentration and I had a couple of races that didn't go well, they were history. I'd dump any girlfriend whom I didn't think made me go faster!

I realized that if people treated me that way I wouldn't like it, so what I really needed to do was learn about relationships. I thought, *I have always been focused on race cars and engineering and goals and just my own selfish motives. How can I learn how to just enjoy being with people and give people time?*

I soon saw that for me, developing relationships with people, especially people I didn't want to know, was *way* harder than anything I'd ever tried to do in a race car. I really had a hard time, having spent all that time being so focused, now trying to see if I could just develop basic social relationships. So I thought, *Can I think of anybody on the racing circuit who thinks more about what other people do, or builds good relationships, or is the type of person whom I might be able to learn something from?*

The guy that I came up with was Hunter Floyd.

The funny thing was, I had no idea what Hunter did. I knew that Hunter was the chaplain for the Indy Car circuit. I knew that as soon as I started the Indy Light Series he would say a prayer at the beginning of the drivers' meeting. And when I got into Indy cars, he would say a prayer at the beginning of each Indy Car drivers' meeting. I never thought much about it beyond noticing his prayers that we would use our God-given abilities the best that we could, that we would stay safe, that we would have good sportsmanship, and that we would conduct ourselves in a way that would give glory to the Lord.

As a driver, that sounded fine to me. That's about all I knew.

The Jasper Motorsports #77 team, featuring driver (and co-owner Bobby Hillin), repeatedly proved that Christian principles are compatable with sustained excellence in <u>any</u> profession.

The eye-catching Pennzoil #21 wins a photo finish with a determined competitor in an early Indy Car race — while <u>averaging</u> a whopping 231.37 miles per hour for the '96 season.

Driver Phil Parsons has enjoyed success in both the NASCAR and Busch Grand National circuits. In 1996, he drove the powder blue CHANNELLOCK #10 to an impressive ninth place finish in the final Busch point standings.

PHOTO BY ERNIE MACHE

While the Interstate Batteries #18 finished further back in the pack in 1996's final point standings than expected, it is dangerous to <u>ever</u> underestimate owner (and former NFL great) Joe Gibbs!

PHOTO BY C.I.A. STOCK PHOTOGRAPHY

Michael Waltrip was behind the wheel of the stunning red/orange Citgo #21 as it roared an impressive 16th place finish in the final NASCAR point standings for 1996.

Jeff Gordon's multi-colored Dupont Motor Refinishes #24 is all but a blur as the head "Rainbow Warrior" zooms his way to one of his 10 victories during the 1996 NASCAR season.

The menacing metallic green of the Remington #75 car took Morgan Shepherd to a number of strong finishes in 1996 and will host veteran Rick Mast in '97.

The father/son team of Joe and Jason Keller own and operate the striking Slim Jim #57 Monte Carlo. Both Kellers started on dirt bikes before moving in karts and — eventually — the Busch Grand Nationals.

Jeff Gordon's rainbow-hued Monte Carlo is shown in its usual position during 1996 — leading the pack — enroute to nearly $2.5 million in earnings and a second-place in the final NASCAR point standings.

Early morning at the state-of-the-art Jasper Motorsports shop north of Charlotte, the bodies of Bobby Hillin's red, white, and blue Thunderbirds patiently wait for the mechanics to arrive.

The tough Pagan Racing/Pennzoil #21 makes a frantic pit stop during an Indy Car race while driver Roberto Guerrero impatiently waits inside.

The brilliant Pennzoil #21, a 1995 Reynard/Ford Cosworth driven by Roberto Guerrero, leads the pack in a late-season Indy Car race.

Featuring a crack crew headed by crew chief Jimmy Makar, the Interstate Batteries #18 hurls towards the flag in late 1996.

Jason Keller and the brilliant Slim Jim #57 Monte Carlo finished an impressive sixth in the final Busch Grand National point standings.

The muscular 1937 Ford Coupe #17k, driven by Kevin Conway, won 11 of 16 races in the Legends Pro division in 1996.

*Up and coming driver Hut Stricklin pushed the brightly colored Circuit City #8
hard during 1996 and nearly won a couple of key races before
eventually finishing 22nd in the final NASCAR
point standings.*

*This Kodiak #41 car carried driver Ricky Craven to a fine
16th place finish in 1996 and will host hot newcomer
Steve Grissom in 1997.*

Bobby Labonte drove the striking Interstate Batteries #18 Monte Carlo to victory in the final race of 1996, the NAPA 500 in Atlanta.

Kevin Conway's fluorescent 1937 Ford Coupe was one of the dominant cars on the Legends circuit, setting track records at Charlotte Motor Speedway and Southside Motor Speedway, and qualifying for the pole at the BF Goodrich National Championships.

The Wood Brothers/Citgo #21, driven by Michael Waltrip, won The Winston Select NASCAR race in Charlotte on May 18, 1996.

I figured it must be Indy Car tradition for the chaplain to come in and give a prayer for Indy Lights and then for Indy Car, but I never really thought about what he did on the circuit other than funerals and weddings.

For me to go to Hunter Floyd was a really big thing. I said, "Okay, who's the person on the circuit who has always been nice to me but has never asked me for anything in return?" As an Indy Car driver, I found people always wanted something. Hunter was the only person I could think of who would come up to me each and every race and ask me how I was doing. He was a former driver himself, and he actually took the time to read the press notes, and he would say, "Jon, I understand you ran third this morning, but I read that it looked like your car had a little bit of understeer. What are you guys doing to fix it?" He was always interested in me and asked me how I was doing.

I decided Hunter had been a good friend to me for three years, so I was going to just go to one of his chapel services. Not because I needed to go there, but because I wanted to thank him for being my friend. *And* I wanted to learn about what it's like to do things for people just because you like them and not because you want something from them. I thought that was what I was missing.

I went to that chapel service, and Hunter talked about a relationship with Christ. He also talked about relationships with other people. I thought, *I've got to find out more about this: not only relationships with other people, but a relationship with our Creator. I think that's what I'm missing.*

I was scared to death somebody might see me talking to the chaplain. I thought that as soon as any of my competitors saw me, they would think that I obviously had some kind of problem or I was worried about something, which would be a sign of weakness.

So I started hiding behind the trailers, asking Hunter all these questions about what it was like to be a Christian and what it really meant. I asked him about a hundred questions, and he took the time to answer them the best he could.

Then he gave me Josh McDowell's book *More Than a Carpenter*, which basically walked me through with an analytical approach to the question, "Is Jesus liar, lunatic, or Lord?"

I got to the end of that book and said, "I don't know why, but

I know this is the truth." I got on my knees and said a prayer. I didn't tell anybody. I did it in the privacy of my own home after I'd probably gone to two or three chapel services of Hunter's. Just before the final race of the season, I prayed the prayer and I asked Jesus to come into my life, to change it. I said, "I'm giving You the steering wheel, and I'm going to commit to this relationship—even though I've never committed fully to anything in the way of relationships."

After becoming a Christian, every Indy Car race that I did, I either ended up on fire, in the hospital, or with a broken car! At last I said, "Okay—I gave my life to Christ and now everything is going in the toilet. So what do I do? Do I get rid of this relationship or do I stick with it?"

Still, I was very committed for the first time to something other than racing. I just knew in my heart that I needed to stay committed to this relationship to the Lord, that there was a reason for this happening.

Things got worse. We could not find sponsorship for the next year, my girlfriend decided that she didn't want to see me anymore, and I got stiffed a year's pay, so I got paid nothing at all for anything I did in 1990.

I could not understand why God was taking all these things away from me. At Hunter's suggestion, I went to the pro athlete's outreach conference. This particular conference was tailored toward racing, so there were a lot of NASCAR people there, a lot of people I had watched before but never met.

What I learned there from Walt Wiley, the chaplain for the Atlanta Braves, was the character of God. He started talking about God being omniscient and omnipresent and all-powerful. He talked about predestination, and he talked about the fact that God knows the beginning and the end and everything in between. This was a totally new concept for me. He described it as our seeing one frame of a movie at a time, whereas God can stretch the film out on a wall and see any frame at any time He chooses.

All of a sudden a light went on. Here I was thinking that God had taken away my racing and that all these bad things were happening because I had become a Christian. Then I realized that God already knew that all these things were going to happen! That's when I started to really see how He came and rattled my cage right when He needed to. I saw that God already knew that all these things were going to happen around October 1990, and they were going to be devastating for me. He wanted to make sure that I had a personal relationship with Him *before* they happened so that I would have something more important in my life when everything started to unravel. That's when I first started to understand about how much He loves me, that He really wants to have a personal relationship with me to comfort me during these times.

I committed to Bible study and to reading and growing. I figured I had to make up for lost time. I approached my Christianity with the same kind of zeal that I had had all those years previously in trying to drive fast in a race car. I was still driving on occasion, but every time I got in a car, something terrible happened.

For instance, on a practice session at the Michigan 500, I went into the third corner at over 200 mph. The nose and the right front wheel hit the wall first, the wheel came back into the car and broke the car in half—not so much broke it, but kinked it, almost like what you could do with an aluminum can.

Of course, I was in the middle of that, and as the car kinked, it broke my right hand and kind of took my legs and stuck them in the crease of where the kink was. It knocked me out, so I was unconscious but—praise the Lord—they *still* can't figure out how it didn't break my legs! It took them about twenty-five minutes to cut me out of the car and relieve the pressure. It felt like my legs were in a vise for twenty-five minutes.

That was an accident where I could have easily been killed and I felt the Lord had really protected me. The first person I saw when they loaded me into the ambulance was Hunter. Hunter rode with me to the hospital and notified my parents. It was such a comfort to have the guy who had led me to the Lord there in the ambulance.

In 1991 I had an opportunity to work for ESPN, not just for Indy Lights coverage, but to do Indy Car coverage in the pits. That was my start. I never really put any feelers out, never did much to try and get something going in television because that was not my goal. I just wanted to be a driver. The only reason I did television at first was because they would pay me to go and cover the races—then I could be there and bug these team owners for a chance to drive their cars. And then all of a sudden I was announcing all these races for television.

From the beginning of '91 on, everything I did in television seemed to be blessed, and everything I did behind the wheel of a race car seemed to be cursed. So after two years of ending up in the hospital and having cars break right and left, I started to get the picture that the Lord was showing me: He had another direction that He wanted me to go in.

Meanwhile, as I read about baptism in the Bible, I realized that Jesus was roughly thirty years old when He was baptized. I decided that on my thirty-first birthday, which was March 31, 1991, I would be baptized. For the first time in my life, that day fell on Easter. So on Easter Sunday, on my thirty-first birthday, Hunter Floyd baptized me in the Carmel River, near Carmel, California.

I feel as though March 31 was the start of my real commitment. I know I was saved prior to that, but that was my real proclamation of faith—and that's when my life *really* started!

GARY BROOKS

Shop Foreman
#2
Penske Racing South
Miller Racing Ford Thunderbird

Rusty Wallace may drive the sinister black Miller Racing Thunderbird, but Gary Brooks keeps it humming. Just forty years old, Gary's already been on the All-Pro teams a whopping nine times in eight years. Not that the years haven't taken their toll: He was a member of the "over-the-wall" gang until back injuries forced his "retirement" to shop foreman in 1993. In March 1996, he underwent two major surgeries on the same day—and was back, full force, in less than two weeks.

The veteran fabricator and mechanic is also known as the Penske Racing team's most compulsive practical joker, providing the usually serious (and almost always successful) #2 team's shop with a pleasant, productive atmosphere.

I came from a Christian background. When I was growing up, my father was a deacon in the church. Every Saturday night we were up there turning the heat on for Sunday services, doing whatever needed to be done. My family was real active in the Southern Baptist church. I grew up in Royal Ambassadors.

At a pretty young age I accepted Christ. I went up in front of the church; I can still remember the night I did it. Everybody kept expecting me to go do it, but I just wasn't ready. I kept feeling the pressure, with everybody looking at me every week thinking, *Are you going?* The preacher even came and talked to me at the house.

After I accepted Christ, I did real well—but I was young too. I knew He was in my heart, but like a lot of people, I made a lot of mistakes. As I got older I kind of went to church on Sundays but did things you weren't supposed to do the other days. I got to running around with the wrong crowd. I still tried to go to church—I had enough in my heart so that when Sunday came I felt like I needed to be in church, but from Monday through Saturday, I didn't live it.

I never grew completely away from the church. The background I had from my mom and dad kept me there. As I got older, though, my mom and dad started getting sick. Virgie and Billy Brooks both died from cancer within seven months.

My mom was a real good Christian lady. Never did anything wrong that I'm aware of. She was always doing something for people. But when my mom really got sick and we found out what was going on, through all of her sickness, she never doubted the Lord. Even when she was lying there dying of cancer and she knew there was nothing they could do for her, we sat and talked at night. She told me, "Never forget me, but I'm going to see the Lord. I'll be there."

My mom and dad worked hard all their lives, never had anything. Before he died, my dad said, "If anything ever happens to me, I've got a toolbox upstairs with some money in it." There was just enough money to get him buried. Pretty much everything else that he did have, we had to sell to pay liens on everything. But he was a hard worker and he was honest. And he was happy. I was real proud of him.

When I was a kid growing up, I played baseball, football, whatever. Dad was always there, no matter what I played. Even if I was the worst player there and sat on the bench, I turned around and he was there.

When my mom died, it was a hard time. But I turned around and my dad was there. But when he died and I turned around, neither one of them was there. That's when I realized, *Okay, you're on your own. You've got to do what they showed you.*

When my mom and my dad were lying on their deathbeds and never doubted Christ, that's when I started coming back. In their final days, both said things like, "The Lord's going to walk with me through this. He's right here." That's when I decided there was a lot more to the Christian faith than just saying "okay." That's when I really started trying to change my life back around and saying, "I've *got* to go this way."

Today, years later, I'm married to my beautiful wife, Terri, with two kids, Colby and Cameron. Today, I know death is a part of life. The Lord has let me enjoy my life, and my day will come. It's inevitable. The only thing that you can do is live your life so that when that time comes, you're ready. With the way the world is getting nowadays, just riding down the road you can get hit by a car and get killed. You don't ever know. The Lord doesn't tell you what day it's going to be and doesn't guarantee you the next minute. So if I were to fall over right now, I hope I'm going to heaven.

And that's the way I try to live my life. I know that I'm a sinner, and I ask for His forgiveness, and that's the best thing I can do. That's the whole thing in a nutshell.

Memorable Moment

When I started racing, I worked for a smaller team, Lenny Pond's. In high school, I'd go over and do whatever they told me.

Then, as I got out of high school, I tried racing myself. That was probably my most exciting time because I wanted to be a driver. But I just didn't ever make it. My dad and mom would sit in the stands every night. I raced on Fridays, Saturdays, and Sunday afternoons. That was a real exciting time for me because I enjoyed driving. I wish I could have made it; I tried as hard as I could. It just didn't work out.

I went back to work for Lenny on his own independent deal. I had a good time working there. We never won any races, never even came close. A lot of the guys who worked there were volunteers. Everybody worked hard; you were all reaching for the same goal. Whatever it took to try to go and win a race, you worked night and day.

When Lenny's deal folded up, the guy who jacked the car for him, my friend Junior, told me, "Listen, I've already got a room in

Daytona. Lenny's not going now that we don't have any car. But I'm still going—do you want to go?"

I said, "I can't afford to go, Junior."

Junior said, "Tell you what, I'm going anyway, I've got a room. You can stay in my room, sleep on the floor, do whatever you want to do. We'll go to Daytona anyway."

I said, "Well, I don't have any money." He said, "I'll lend you two hundred dollars and you can ride with me, I'll pay for the gas, and you can sleep on the floor."

I said, "Let's go."

So we went to Daytona, and I walked around in the garage area. Back then it wasn't quite as elaborate as it is now. Today people have résumés drawn up and are college educated. Not me. I went down there, went to the drugstore, bought one of those little spiral-back notebooks. I wrote my name, my address, and my phone number on each page. I walked around through the garage area going, "Hi, I'm Gary Brooks," and handed them a sheet of paper. "I'm looking for a job." Some of them threw it in the trash can as soon as I walked off, some of them stuck it in their pocket and went on, some remembered me from working with Lenny. I went through two or three of those little notebooks the whole week. Didn't hear a thing.

We came back and I went to Richmond to the race with my dad. Meanwhile, J. D. Stacy had just bought out Rod Osturland. Robert Harrington was going to be the team manager and Dale Inman at Petty Enterprises had come down. As we were standing there on the guardrail, Robert came over to me and said, "Are you still looking for a job?"

I said, "Yes, sir!"

He said, "When can you come to work?"

This was on a Saturday. I said, "Monday morning."

He said, "Be in Alton, North Carolina, on Monday morning at 8 A.M."

I left home the next day in a '73 Hornet station wagon. Didn't even own a suitcase. I had five grocery bags full of clothes, two five-gallon buckets, some fishing poles, and about $110 in my pocket. And down the road I went.

I started to work for them, and we ran pretty good there. That was my first big break, and I'll always remember that.

JOE GIBBS

Owner
#18
Joe Gibbs Racing
Interstate Batteries Monte Carlo

Few people have a chance to become legends in one sport. Fewer still get to do it in two. Joe Gibbs is one of those rare individuals. As head coach of professional football's Washington Redskins for twelve seasons, he won 140 games, went to four Super Bowls (winning three), and was inducted into the Pro Football Hall of Fame in 1996.

Since coming to NASCAR in the early nineties as a team owner, Joe's success has been nearly as dramatic. In only his second year, he won the Daytona 500 (NASCAR's version of the Super Bowl), and in 1995 the team won a staggering $1.4 million, courtesy of three wins and two poles.

Along the way he's found time to become a successful author and a greatly in-demand motivational speaker.

Today, Joe Gibbs is still ramrod straight, as lean as a marine, and as unswerving in his service to his God as ever.

Still, it's significant that his #18 Monte Carlo is the only one on the NASCAR circuit that proudly displays the NFL Properties logo!

I grew up in the hills of North Carolina, and I had a mother and a grandmother who kept me in church when I was young. I went to church for Bible school, Sunday school—I was *always* in and out of church.

I think, through their influence and being exposed to the Bible, that I finally came to this conclusion when I was only nine years old: "Look, I've got two choices here. One, I can believe what I'm being told in school, which is that two amoeba hit a puddle of muddy water a couple of million years ago and I'm an accident. Or two, there's a God who created me and loves me. Hey! That makes a lot more sense to me!" It is very obvious to me that there is a God when you look at the world and the way it is made and the way we are made.

My pastor, my grandmother, and my mother encouraged me to read the Bible. This became my second bit of proof that God exists. Think about it—so far, everything in it, from the beginning to the end, has been perfect. You know how hard that is? As a coach, I've had to call plays from the press box by telling an assistant coach who told a player who eventually told the quarterback. It's next to impossible to get the message right! Imagine thirty-five men over a period of fifteen hundred years writing the same thing about God. The Bible is truth, plain and simple. God created Adam and Eve, and you and me, for a purpose. He wants to have a relationship with us.

It was at that time, age nine, that I trusted Christ as my Savior and Lord. I went forward in church and I always went to church after that. Then there was a period of time after high school where I drifted away from the Lord. As I grew older, I found that there were other things the world wanted me to believe. One was that you only have one life to live, and then you die. And that's all there is. Because of that, you should do your own thing, whatever it takes, to live a happy and successful life.

As my coaching career took off, I bought right into the world's game plan. I wanted to be a head coach. In my eyes, that would give me all the things, like money and prestige, I wanted and thought I needed. It became an obsession. I wanted to be a head coach more than anything.

I bounced around from one assistant job to another and in 1972, while coaching at the University of Arkansas, God put me around a group of people in Fayetteville, Arkansas. I had a Sunday school teacher there who became my spiritual father—George

Tharel. I was intrigued by him, as much by his life as his teaching. He was a man at peace with himself and with God. Being driven was one of my strengths, but I envied people who could relax and enjoy life.

Looking at George's life, I started to see that there was another game plan besides the world's. God's plan was not based on money, position, or winning football games. God was only concerned with my having a right relationship with Him. Even though I had become a Christian as a nine-year-old, I had never made God a priority. George helped me see that.

At the same time, there were some other people on the coaching staff at the University of Arkansas like Raymond Berry, Don Breaux, and others. God enabled me to see how they were living and how *I* was living. Through the influence of a lot of people, it became obvious to me that I was not living a committed Christian life.

Finally, I went forward in church one night and rededicated my life to Christ. I confessed in my heart, saying, "God, I've known You since I was nine years old, but I have not been living for You. Tonight, I want to rededicate and commit my life to You."

As I began to live that out, it became evident that my life was different. Some of the changes were immediate, but others have been a process.

One major process God took me through was being able to trust Him with my career. I had wanted to be a head coach for so long. That had been my drive, my goal. Giving that desire over to the Lord didn't come easily. At times, I wanted to be a head coach more than I wanted God or even my family. It was during one of those times that God began to change my heart.

In 1978, my first year as the offensive coordinator for the Tampa Bay Buccaneers, I just knew I was one step away from being a head coach. That was until we finished the season four and twelve—the first unsuccessful program I'd ever been a part of. After that season, Don Coryell got the head job with the Chargers, and I prayed, "Lord, don't have him call me unless You want me to go."

Don called me the next day and offered me a job. The only problem was that the job was not as the offensive coordinator. I would have to be a backfield coach. My pride got in the way, and it really bothered me. I prayed about it and took the job, but I had no peace about it.

So, I decided to see George back in Arkansas. I got on a plane, but a snowstorm prevented me from making it to Fayetteville. I asked God, "Why? Why are You doing this to me?" After we got back to the airport in Fort Smith, I noticed a Bible sitting around, so I picked it up and turned to the first chapter of James. Out of nowhere, a guy about my age tapped me on the shoulder and said, "I claimed those verses in that chapter about six months ago."

I said, "Really?"

And without me saying a word, this guy rattled off a story that paralleled mine almost exactly! He had the job he'd always wanted, lost it, and tried everything he could to get it back. Then God, in His timing, gave it back to him. This was no coincidence! God brought this guy into my life to show me what I needed to do.

After boarding the plane, I prayed, "God, all my life I've wanted to be a head football coach, but I'm putting my career in Your hands."

I went to San Diego and within two weeks, the offensive coordinator left, opening the position for me. Two years later, I became the head coach of the Washington Redskins.

Memorable Moment

My first impulse is to say that winning the Daytona 500 is that moment. But each one of our wins was monumental for me. When you win a race and there are forty other competitors competing, that's tough! So I cherish each one of those.

Just as in football, when you're asked to name your most memorable victories it is hard to pick one out. I will have to say that winning even one Daytona 500 is certainly a highlight. But on second thought, I think the Charlotte 600, where Bobby Labonte won his first race—I'd have to rate those experiences dead even. Part of it was that it was so emotional since it was Bobby's first win and he'd originally come to our race team without a win in Winston Cup. It was a big race, it was at home—it was just big.

The Daytona 500, of course, was our first victory as a team—and it was in the Super Bowl of NASCAR! It was our second year as a racing team, and we hadn't won anything yet. It had been a tough year, so that made it all the more special to all of us.

DOUG BAWEL

Owner
#77
Jasper Engines/Federal Mogul
Jasper Motorsports Ford Thunderbird

Doug Bawel is president and part-owner of Jasper Engines & Transmissions, a company that develops engines and drivetrains for NASCAR Winston Cup cars. In 1993, Doug and partners Mark Wallace and Mark Harrah purchased D. K. Ulrich's interest in Jasper Motorsports. Three years later, they brought driver Bobby Hillin aboard as a part-owner as well.

Doug is committed to the concept of a company operated on Christian principles. Copies of the corporate statement of Christian principles are posted everywhere. Both the Indiana and North Carolina offices have numerous Bible studies. And all employees receive full pay for the days they voluntarily participate in one of the Christian renewal seminars, Cursillo or Walk to Emmaus.

But Doug doesn't offer his executive committee a similar option. "They can either go on a Walk or a Cursillo," he said. "Some say, 'What if we don't want to go?' I say, 'That's not an option. The option is either one or the other—you pick which one you want. But my pledge to you is, if you finish and you feel that the weekend was not beneficial to you, you tell me what weekend, what activity, you've done that is better—and you and I will go on that together, my treat.'

"Well, since then, I've never had to take anyone anywhere."

■ 99 ■

came from a Christian family, and I was raised in the church. I was an adult Sunday school teacher. I attended regularly with my family. But I got caught up in the so-called "worldly" ways.

That didn't change until I attended a Walk to Emmaus—Catholics have the Cursillo and the ecumenical movement has its Walk to Emmaus. And during that weekend I took Jesus Christ as my personal Savior. Even though I'd taught Sunday school, knew that God and Jesus existed, I felt they were Somebody who should stay in church. It was great to go there on Sundays and feel that feeling—but then we had to go back into the real world Monday through Saturday.

That week on the Walk, I listened to a speaker. The talk was on priorities. I had a lot of goals. I had set a goal to be a president of a company by age thirty-five; I wanted to own my own business by age forty. I'd met most of those goals. But along the way, I had lost a relationship with two daughters. We were close, but work came first and my family came second. I was always able to reconcile it because they wanted dance lessons and Dad was a good provider. Or they wanted the finer things in life, and Dad was a good provider. And I always took them to Sunday school, and we always went to church.

But I missed a few of those dance recitals. And everything else.

So during the Walk, another individual talked about going through a divorce. And I was going through a divorce at the time. His comment was, "Later in life, after you have all of the worldly possessions, as you grow old, as you get ready for that Day of Judgment—how will you fare?" Then he asked, "How will you fare with your family?"

That was a pretty tough question. So during the next few minutes, after the talk, we discussed what it meant to each of the men at our table.

One of the posters the speaker used showed the reverse of the word *Jesus*. Perhaps you've seen it: It's a bit of calligraphy where the shape *between* letters spells out the word. It's like an optical illusion. But I couldn't see the word *Jesus* no matter how many times I tried.

Afterward we had a break and I found myself in the chapel. I sat in a pew and there was the same banner on the altar. And I still couldn't see the word *Jesus*. I kept thinking, *You know, I'm not that bright, but I'm not that stupid, either! I've got to be able to figure out how to see that word in reverse.*

It just so happened that this church had Bibles in every pew. I opened one at random and landed on John 8, the story of the woman who'd committed adultery. And Jesus said to the people around them, "He who is without sin among you, let him throw a stone at her first. . . . Then those who heard it, being convicted by their conscience, went out one by one, beginning with the oldest even to the last."

It was at that moment that I turned to the Lord. I said, "You know, I've kept You on a shelf for too many years. I feel this terrible weight of the world on my shoulders. I finally submit to You."

At the time, my life was going along quite well—or so I thought. But as I looked up, after I'd said my little prayer, I could read the word *Jesus* very plainly!

Of course, being somewhat like doubting Thomas, I closed one eye. Gosh, I could see it with that eye. So I closed the other eye and I could still see it!

About thirty minutes had elapsed by this point and one of the clergy came in and quietly tapped me on the shoulder and asked, "Are you okay?"

I said, "I can see the word *Jesus*!"

He said, "Uh, we *all* can."

I said, "No, *I* can see it!"

That began my walk with the Lord. That was some six years ago.

Since that time, my life has become extremely abundant. My daughters and I not only patched together our relationship, but they've moved in with me. I met and married another Christian lady, Kathy, and we ended up adopting another child, getting her involved in church, and she accepted Christ in her life.

My wife and I have also worked to establish a teens movement called Chrysalis. It's a division of the Walk to Emmaus for young people. We went off to be trained, came back, and organized the first one in our hometown.

Everyone said that would be a tough time in our lives. And,

boy, was it ever. I remember leaving on Thanksgiving Day to go off to a training session and Kathy saying, "Gee whiz, is this really what the Lord wants? You're not home that much and you're leaving again."

Six weeks before the weekend all of the young people were to arrive, my daughter Lori, who is blind in one eye, went blind in the other eye. We took her to a number of doctors, and they couldn't figure out what the problem was.

That was also the first year I'd become a part-owner in a Winston Cup team. It just so happened that the weekend of Chrysalis was going to be the weekend of the Daytona 500.

So here I'm part-owner of a Winston Cup team, I can't make the Daytona race, Chrysalis is coming up, and my daughter is unable to see.

We decided to go only for the testing at Daytona and return home in time for Chrysalis. Lori flew down with me because she's always been involved in the sport. And on the way to the track, she said, "We're on Richard Petty Boulevard." Her eyesight had returned!

It was just a test, I think, to see if I was willing to give up racing for these young people. Incidentally, Lori still has sight in one eye and is doing quite well. She's become very active in the church and the Chrysalis movement.

Memorable Moment

Outside of Lori's miracle, there have probably been two. One is our involvement with MRO. We've had the opportunity to hear some great speakers, sermons, and testimonies. It has really strengthened the belief my wife and I have that doing it right is the right way. It's so easy to get off base, to get drawn into this mind-set: "Well, it's Sunday, we've got sponsors to deal with, and we can skip church." So we tell our sponsors up front: "That's a special time and we'll work up to 10 A.M. But from 10 A.M. on, we want to be in the church service." That's been special.

Another moment was at Talladega, Alabama, in 1996. My wife and I missed the race. We stayed and went to church instead. So many people came up and put a hand on my shoulder and said, "Doug, we know it is tough right now, but just hang in there. Don't give up your principles."

When we founded this team, in our corporate statement of principles, paragraph three says that we want to be known as good corporate Christian citizens. That's been tough at times when we've been recruiting people, saying, "These are the principles we're going to live by." But we feel we want to be, and can be, witnesses to racing.

Every Friday, we meet with as many of the original Walk to Emmaus people as we can. There are four of us in the group, although the numbers fluctuate. We meet at lunch and for six years, where more than one meet in the name of the Lord, things happen.

We've carried that a little farther in our company. They caution you when you're on a Walk or Cursillo not to go back to your home and job and talk too much. Let people see your *actions*. But it had such a measurable impact in my life that we had people in my company coming to me and saying, "We've noticed you've changed—what was it?"

We have a prayer line for everyone who goes on the Walk. Participants can check into their voice mail, and any prayer requests we have are automatically linked across that. We also have a lot of prayer groups that meet at our company facility. It's been a real blessing.

We've been accused of not being receptive to all forms of religion. So during the hiring process we say, "These are our beliefs. If you believe in a Higher Power that's different from ours, we respect you for that. But we want you to know where we stand. We're Christ–centered."

JASON KELLER

Driver/Co–Owner
#57
Kel Racing
Slim Jim Racing Team Monte Carlo

For Jason Keller, it has been a sixteen-year overnight success story. It begins with his father, Joe Keller, an avid dirt biker and racer, who fixed up a small motorcycle with training wheels long before Jason could ride a bike. It's been a father/son team ever since.

The two first went into go-Karts when Jason was ten, winning back-to-back national championships in the World Karting Association's Limited Modified class. Jason enjoyed equal success driving for dirt-track legend Jack Finley's #57 in the Super Late Model division.

Even the move to the Winston Racing Series didn't slow down the Keller juggernaut. In 1990, Jason was Rookie of the Year in the All American Challenge Series. The following year, they finished third in the Slim Jim All-Pro Series before moving into the Busch Series full-time.

Today he's a top driver on the Busch circuit, driving the striking red #57 Slim Jim Monte Carlo. But Jason is quick to credit his gene pool when recounting his successes: "I think racing is in my blood. No, I know racing is in my blood."

My mom and dad are very faithful, so I was fortunate to have a Christian upbringing. It helped a lot when I got into trouble sometimes growing up. It was a strong foundation for me.

As a young person, sometimes you take things for granted. As I grew older and faced a lot tougher decisions and tougher roads to travel in my life, I think that's when I reached out and asked for His help to lead me in the right direction—and I've been doing it ever since. I've been very fortunate that I've been able to trust Him and that He's been able to lead me down the right path.

I've also been very fortunate throughout my career to have my family with me. My father and I started this race team back in the mid-1980s when we first started running dirt cars around the Southeast. I had him there for strength. And the more I went on in my profession, I was fortunate enough to have my wife along as well (we married in 1992). I've had a very solid family foundation to fall back on.

This profession is very tough, and if you let it get ahold of you, you find yourself trapped in it and racing for all the wrong reasons: fame and glory. If you're not careful, you'll find yourself racing to overachieve and get stuck in that rut and lose sight of the things that are most important to you.

Through MRO's involvement and Ron and Jackie Pegram, before every race we have a chapel session, and that helps keep everything in perspective. It's a time away from the glitz and glamour of racing. You sit down and you really get one-on-one with the Lord. It's special because if you don't have that quality time, I think you get caught up in racing too much. Through my career, I found myself doing that. But with the help of my family and Ron and Jackie, I've been able to stay on the right track and be focused on my career, but not so focused that I lose sight of the fact of what's important.

Ron and Jackie travel with the Busch Car Series, Grand National division, and they're great. Ron comes by my car before every race and we say a little prayer, not only for me but for all the drivers, that God will keep everyone safe. It really means a lot. We're in the spotlight, but we're human beings too. We have to have things that we can hold on to and feel close to. And one thing I feel good about is my faith and my family upbringing, and Ron keeps me focused on those aspects.

We have weekly sessions every Saturday probably about two hours before the race, usually after the drivers meet, when Ron and

Jackie get us together. Some good things have definitely come out of that. With our busy lifestyles, a lot of times we find ourselves getting too busy or too wrapped up in things. With Ron and Jackie, you know they're going to be there. It's a time to get away from the autograph sessions and things of that nature and just go and share your faith with each other and enjoy being together.

Coming up through my career, I've been very successful very quickly in most of the steps that I've taken. But in 1993, when I first started trying to come into the Busch Grand National Series, it was real tough. You fail to qualify for races, and you wonder if you're in the right profession. You wonder if you're doing the right thing, and you wonder if it's even worth it. You just keep struggling and struggling and struggling. It seems like it's a never-ending battle.

In 1993 I really had to sit down and take a close look and ask the Lord to lead me down the path that He wanted me to go on. Luckily, it's worked out that racing has been the path that He's chosen for me. I'm going down that path now, and I'm going down it in His will—and that's the way I want to do it.

Any professional athlete, be it basketball, football, golf, or whatever, is looked up to a little bit more. If you're in the spotlight more and you're on TV more, people are going to idolize what you do. I think that showing a good Christian upbringing and lifestyle can be very influential.

On the other hand, I think that being a professional athlete can be very negative. You see a lot of professional athletes in the different sports getting hooked on drugs and getting locked up because of drugs. These are the type of people that children and even adults idolize. It's very disheartening to see these kinds of things.

Fortunately, I think it's very uncommon to see these kinds of things in racing. If you go around the racetrack, nine times out of ten you see the drivers with their wives and children. It's a very close-knit family. We're very lucky to be in the profession and at the level we're in.

My wife and I have a motor home now, so we're getting a lot closer to a lot of the other drivers and their families. It's really nice to have common bonds with these people. Although we race together, it's nice to have something off the track, and we enjoy their kids, the people, and their faith. There are a lot of Christian drivers out there.

More than anything, I try to lead by example. That's the biggest thing. I want for everyone to know that Jason Keller is a straight, good person and a truthful person. I would like to think that I have had some influence in helping some people to stay focused in their direction, not letting anyone stand in the way of their dreams, to really go down the right path. That's the biggest thing I've discussed with young kids. Last year I got to talk to a group, a Royal Ambassadors group in Darlington, and I think there were about eight hundred kids there. I hope that I helped one or two of them to stay focused and, no matter how hard it is, to trust in themselves and know that the Lord will lead them down the right path.

You see, you have to trust Him because at the racetracks we run, you're going at very high speeds. You have to trust Him to watch over you and that you'll do the right things and make the right decisions during the race. Our profession is so fast-paced, so flamboyant, you can't be calm and peaceful. You have to be aggressive, and sometimes you step over the line of being aggressive. You just have to know in yourself that you're doing the right thing, and everything else will take care of itself.

Memorable Moment

The biggest highlight I've ever had in my racing career was the race in 1995 that I won at Indianapolis Raceway Park. I sat there and cried in Victory Lane because it was something special. My dad and I had built this race team from scratch. We didn't go out and buy a race team. We didn't go out and buy me a position on a race team. We *built* the race team, and to win a race at a major level, it was really special. To have both my wife and my dad in Victory Lane with me was even more special. I can say we shed a lot of tears in Victory Lane that day!

MICHAEL WALTRIP

Driver
#21
Wood Brothers
Citgo Ford Thunderbird

Michael Waltrip left the popular Bahari Racing team at the end of the 1995 season and joined the legendary Wood Brothers with their bright red Citgo #21 in early 1996. And to the surprise of absolutely no one, the results were much the same: continued, sustained racing success.

Darrell Waltrip's younger brother promptly enjoyed yet another notable season, continuing his streak of Winston Cup consecutive starts (number 300 was the 1996 Daytona 500), racking up a fistful of top-ten finishes, and winning the all-star Winston Select race in Charlotte (after starting in the twentieth and last position).

Michael dominated the old NASCAR Dash Series in the '80s, won seven Busch Grand National races, and has career earnings of nearly $5 million in motor racing to date.

But it hasn't changed the tall, affable Waltrip. He admitted that his favorite verse still remains Philippians 4:6: "Be anxious for nothing, but in everything by prayer and supplication, with thanksgiving, let your requests be made known to God."

By the time I came along, my family was no longer active in church. My family went to church only irregularly, so I didn't learn a whole lot about the Bible or the Lord when I was growing up. It wasn't until I got older that I started to be more curious and started to learn more.

I guess I was about fourteen or fifteen. I had some friends, the people who lived across the street from us, who went to church a lot. They were a Christian family, and I started going to church with them a little bit. Along the way, they explained to me that if you ask the Lord to come into your heart and live there, He will help you make the decisions about what is right or wrong, and you will be forgiven for the sins that you've committed and would commit.

I thought that sounded like a pretty neat deal! So I did. I guess just wanting to know more is how I came to know the Lord. I felt the Lord wanting to come inside of me, making me wonder, making me yearn to ask more questions, and learn more answers. And the friends whom I was fortunate enough to surround myself with then were a Christian family, and they helped guide me to the Lord. And now, I know that every decision that I make, He is in my heart, guiding me.

Still, sometimes it's difficult, but as I said: He's always there for me. That reminds me and helps me through the hard times because I try to base all of my decisions and the things I do on what I think the Lord would want me to do.

I was always racing and traveling a lot, and so I didn't get to attend a church on a regular basis because the races were usually on Saturday or Sunday. We're fortunate out here in NASCAR to have Motor Racing Outreach (MRO). They get up a great church service every Sunday and Bible study nearly every Saturday night. They also provide wonderful counseling and support. They're responsible for a lot of people growing in the Lord.

Does the danger in motor racing impact how drivers live their lives?

It doesn't affect me. I don't look at it that way. I just figure that I'm a pretty smart race car driver and I'm driving the safest cars in the whole world. There are going to be chances for death in anything you do. Whether you're a golfer or a baseball player or a football player or a race car driver, there are ways you could die in and out of your sport. If I thought I was driving something that was going to kill me, I'd quit.

My faith may not impact what I do so much on the racetrack, but I really think it does off the racetrack. Our sport is *very* competitive. It's real tense at times, so it is nice to have Max Helton and the MRO staff around when you have questions or when you're having a hard time. And generally, no matter what problem you have, God can help you with it and make it better. That helps me more than anything.

Do you pray during a race?

Not during the actual laps when I'm racing, but all the time before the race and before qualifying and definitely under caution flags! You just mainly seek reassurance. You can't really talk to anybody much out there—you have radios, but those are for talking to the crew about the car. But when God's with you, you can talk to Him *any* time and it always feels good. Mostly it is just whispered prayers to keep us safe. But I always ask Him to let me do the very best that I possibly can with the ability He's given me. If I do that in a day's race, I know I've done all I can do.

Memorable Moment

My entire racing career has gone fairly well. I haven't enjoyed as much success as I would obviously like to, but I've always been real competitive and won a few big races. I'm certainly not going to complain about my career because I feel that I'm at a point in time where the best is still ahead of me. So I'm pretty happy with the way it has all gone, and I'm still enjoying what I do.

Like many of the guys, I started out with small, underfinanced teams and raced that way for two or three years. Reflecting on those years, I have to say the fact that I survived them and was able to get from race to race, doing well enough that I kept a ride—that allows me to race today, and that's probably the biggest miracle God's ever worked in my life!

One victory was real special to me. That was when I won a Grand National race in Bristol, Tennessee, and in Victory Lane I proposed to my wife (Elizabeth)—that was pretty neat.

It was also the first race after our Winston Cup Champion

Alan Kulwicki died in a plane crash. I did the first ever "Polish Victory Lap" in his honor afterward. When Alan, who was Polish, would win a race, he would drive around the racetrack the wrong direction.

I'd had the engagement ring for some time, but you can't hardly plan to win races! Actually, I plan to win them all, but it doesn't seem to work very well. But we were fortunate enough to win that day, and it just seemed like the time to propose with everybody watching and on TV!

JIMMY MAKAR

Crew Chief
#18
Joe Gibbs Racing
Interstate Batteries Monte Carlo

True race fans, of course, will immediately recognize Jimmy Makar (they'll also know it is pronounced May-car) as crew chief or mechanic with numerous highly successful teams and drivers: Rusty Wallace, Blue Max, the late Tim Richmond, and the Roger Penske teams of the early '90s.

Joe Gibbs is a true race fan too. When he formed his own racing team, the first thing he did was hire Jimmy, 1988's TRW Mechanic of the Year. In 1996, Gibbs signed Jimmy and driver Bobby Labonte to five-year contracts, something virtually unheard of in NASCAR. That security is a long way from the eight thousand dollars a year he once made as a fabricator for Richard Gee.

And he'll need it. Jimmy and his wife, Patti, had twin sons on August 19, 1994!

I didn't really come from a Christian family. When I was a kid, my parents weren't real churchgoing folks. They belonged to the Ukrainian Catholic church, and the priest came by at Easter and Christmas and blessed the house. But they spoke a lot of the service in Ukrainian, very little in English, so for me, it just slipped by with very little notice. I just didn't get involved.

What got me interested were some things that happened in my life. A close friend of mine whom I met when I first moved to Charlotte to go racing, Raymond Fox, died suddenly of a heart attack. It was pretty hard on me. At the time, I really didn't know Max Helton; he'd just come aboard as chaplain of Motor Racing Outreach. But somebody told him that I had been a real close friend with Rick and that I was taking his death pretty hard. Max just came and talked to me a little bit out of the clear blue. No pressure, no nothing, just a shoulder to cry on. That was my first experience talking with someone in the Christian faith. Some other things started happening, some different things, and Max always seemed to be there. He'd always make it a point to come up to me at the racetrack or one day during the week, to ask, "How are you doing?" or "How are things going?" I thought, listening to him talk, *You know, I think I'm going to go to the MRO chapel service this Sunday morning before the race.* Max got me interested. That was the start.

Later, in 1992, when I first talked to Joe Gibbs about joining his team, he knew that I had a pretty wild background. Some of the teams I'd worked on partied hard. At the same time, before I got there, I knew Joe's background as well. I knew he was a Christian; I'd read his book. I'd always thought he was a neat guy. I liked Joe's zest, the way he approached life, the way he approached people. Once I joined the team, I began using Joe as a model. Because of Max and Joe, every day I was getting a little better, learning the Bible a little more.

When the Washington Redskins went to the Super Bowl in Minneapolis in 1992, Joe took some of us along. The Saturday night before the Super Bowl, my wife and I were invited to go to the service for the team. It was a difficult experience for me because up until that point, all I'd really done was attend MRO services. The speaker told a story about a kid growing up in the ghetto and getting into trouble. Suddenly, I realized that the speaker was telling *his* story. *He* was the kid. It just captivated me to listen how this kid had come through life and eventually came to know the Lord. I thought, *Wow! This is really amazing!*

When he was finished, he said, "Will you all bow your heads

with me? And if you haven't come to know Jesus as your personal Savior and you want to accept Him tonight, will you please stand?"

Well, I sat there a while. It was a really weird situation for me, *really* weird. The first time he said it, I didn't think about it. Then he asked the same question a second time, and I started thinking. He asked a *third* time. My hands started sweating. I thought, *Wow! What's going on here?*

He asked a *fourth* time. By now, five minutes into it, it suddenly seemd as if *something* was focusing in on me personally.

I thought, *Jimmy, this isn't going to stop until you do something.* I couldn't move, but the speaker kept on asking. My hands kept sweating. I got to shaking. Finally I thought, *I've got to stand up! I need to stand up and accept Christ.*

When I stood up, not a second passed before I felt my wife, Patti, stand up next to me! That touched me pretty hard.

For some reason, when I looked for her, I saw Dale Jarrett and *his* wife, Kelley, standing up as well! The same thing hit all four of us at the same time!

I accepted Christ in that moment and realized that I needed to learn and to change my lifestyle.

Today, as I think back on it, I realize it was the Holy Spirit working in my life, convicting me to do this. But at the time it was really weird! I can tell people now, "You'll *know* when the Holy Spirit is working in you because it's obvious. It's not a wishy-washy thing. Zoom! It's there!"

At the Super Bowl the next day, the Redskins went on and won the game, and that was a big deal; but my fondest memory is that night before, accepting Christ, and what it has done in my life since.

It has brought me a real peace of mind about the business I'm in, as up and down and traumatic as this business can be. I know there are things I can't handle, that I can't control. It has really made my life a lot more pleasant and a lot more pleasant for the people around me, I feel certain.

And it has been a wonderful growth experience for me. I've met new people, made new friends, learned so much about a better way of living my life and accepting things. It has been a real pleasure knowing Jesus.

Memorable Moment

Three or four key things have happened in my life professionally that have been a big deal. One of the biggest things was back in '87 when, in my current capacity as a chassis guy, working on cars and tuning cars, I was working with Rusty Wallace. He'd just come on board, he was a young kid who hadn't won any races and didn't know anything. We were sort of a ragtag bunch of guys who put together a team called Blue Max Racing. It was owned by a drag racer out of Texas, Raymond Beadle. And it was a fun-loving, wild bunch of guys. But we went to Bristol, Tennessee, and we won Rusty's first race for him! Now that was a real thrill for all of us to win a race *and* win Rusty's first race. And in my capacity as a chassis guy, that was my first big break in racing.

The next would have been when we won the championship with Rusty in 1989. That was another big deal but a lot different from just winning the race. That was a long, drawn-out, everyday experience for eight months. And to finally win the championship—and only nine or ten teams throughout the history of racing have *ever* won it—was quite a feat. And quite rewarding too.

The third thing was winning the Daytona 500 with Dale Jarrett. That was the first deal for us as a team. To be in the biggest race that there is was a phenomenal thing to do and experience. So that was a highlight.

The next biggest thing was to win Bobby Labonte his first race. It makes me really proud to get people their "first" *anything*. It has been so much fun to help Joe Gibbs build a race team and then to make it a winning race team, to make it a success, to get Bobby Labonte his first win, to get Dale his first win with our team—I get a kick out of helping other people achieve things.

You see, we started this team from scratch in 1991. When I walked in the door, it was just a warehouse Joe had bought full of parts. To think back on that and see the state-of-the-art, multimillion-dollar facility here today, I know this really is my baby. To stop and think about that gives me a good feeling. We may be up and down at times, but we've won races, we've won poles, we've had success—and we'll have it again.

LARRY HEDRICK

Owner, Larry Hedrick Motorsports
#41
Larry Hedrick Motorsports
Kodiak Racing
Chevrolet Monte Carlo

Larry Hedrick is the Jerry Clower of motorsports. With his deep drawl and ready wit, Larry has a joke or story for every occasion. And like Clower, that humor stems from a deep and abiding wellspring of Christian faith.

But don't let the good ol' boy facade fool you. Larry's a keen businessman as well. He owns a minor league baseball team, auto dealerships, a holding company, an auction and realty firm, a trading company, and an investment firm.

Still, more often than not, you're likely to find Larry at his high-tech shop, improbably situated in rural North Carolina, kibitzing with the crew and talking strategy with his driver, 1995 Rookie of the Year Ricky Craven.

I came from a Christian home. I was born in 1940, during a time when even in the public schools there was a presence of the Bible. The whole time I was growing up, my parents were very active in church, and I went with them. We had a circuit-rider preacher name Grady White in those days who preached at our church every second and fifth Sunday. We were lucky—sometimes we got him twice in a month!

In the rural area where I grew up there was a program called The Children's Bible Mission that came around to the schools and awarded students for Bible verse memorization. If you memorized, for instance, John 3:16, they gave you the gospel of John. Then there was a schedule of verses you had to learn in a certain sequence to progress from entry level (the gospel of John), to a nice wall plaque with a Scripture reference from the New Testament. Once you memorized enough verses from it, they would give you a Bible. Then you'd start memorizing verses from the Old Testament. And if you did what you were supposed to do, at the end of a certain number of verses—I believe it was three hundred—you would get to go to their summer camp which, at that time, was down in Raleigh, North Carolina.

I finally memorized enough verses to go to camp when I was twelve or thirteen, and it was at one of these camps where I was converted. The camp was not a high-pressure gospel situation. It seemed to me that the way the gospel was presented was extremely clear: All I had to do was believe on the Lord Jesus Christ and I would be saved.

That took place one day. It was really a revelation. It wasn't like, "Yeah, well, okay, I guess I want to come up and make my profession." It wasn't that way at all. I remember the feeling very clearly, even today.

So today I feel that I'm a lot better off. I know *exactly* that I am a Christian. I know *exactly* that I'm not as good a Christian as I ought to be. And I know *exactly* what I must do to continue to be a good Christian. And it's hard to do that, it's just hard. I have nobody to blame for not having the opportunity to be a Christian because my mom and dad did all of the right things. It is still a daily, almost hourly, communication that I have, and will continue to have, with God.

Incidentally, though my wife-to-be, Sue, and I lived in the same rural county, we didn't meet until senior high school. Coincidentally, her family's church was also served by Grady White. He retired before we got married but came out of retirement to marry us.

Sue is the typical country girl who grew up on a dairy farm

and in those days for both of us, the church was the social life. In fact, when it came to baptism in those days, since there was neither indoor plumbing nor a baptistery in our church, we were baptized in the creek. We were not only married by the same preacher, we were baptized by the same preacher in the same creek, although at different times in our lives.

I have and probably always will have some extreme potholes to dodge, but the great thing about it is that as good as I try to be and as good as I think I am, every night I always look over in the bed beside me and there's somebody a heck of a lot better! Sue is my rock.

Memorable Moment

Kodiak Racing has not had any on-track victories yet. But the crash at Talladega in 1995 was an extremely trying and traumatic weekend. Despite Ricky Craven's terrible wreck that day, we still count it as gain because Ricky was spared and delivered to us. After seeing him survive, I believe Ricky has a special future, the purpose of which just hasn't been revealed to us yet.

Generally, during the week, we stand on the top of our trucks to watch races unfold, mostly to determine if our car is pushing or loose or whatever. On race day, when the stands are filled with people, on some tracks the crowd can't see across if people are on their trucks in the infield, so they don't let you sit on the trucks.

But on that Sunday in Talladega, where the track is so long and the distance from side to side is so great, you can't see across anyway. So we could stand atop our trucks and watch during the race. On this day, I was down in the pit area originally but moved to the truck to see better. After about four or five laps, I saw a group of cars coming up all bunched tightly together. I remember thinking, *This is not good. It's too crowded. It looks as though something stupid could happen.*

Two or three laps later, something *did* happen. There was a series of crashes. Since Talladega is 2.66 miles around, it happened nearly three-quarters of a mile away from where we were! I ran to a nearby TV monitor and saw the replay of our car smashing into the fence. Over the radio, I could hear the spotter saying "Ricky! Ricky, are you all right? Ricky, answer me!"

I had to either fight my way to the crash site three-quarters of a mile away and maybe miss him as the emergency teams brought him back, or go to the care center. Well, Ricky's wife, Cathleen, was also in the pit area and she rushed up, along with Charley Pressley, our crew chief. We ran over to the care center. It was thirty to forty minutes before they could extract Ricky from that mangled car and bring him to the care center. During all that time, we had no communication, no indication of how badly he was hurt. We all prayed nonstop.

After about a half hour, the guys who hadn't been trapped started coming in to the center. We asked each one, "Have you seen Ricky?" None of them had. They didn't know any more than we did.

Finally, Ricky was brought in on a stretcher. We could see him feebly moving his arms and legs, but we had no idea how bad the internal injuries were.

The doctor finally came back and told us that they didn't detect any life-threatening injuries, but they were going to have to airlift him to Birmingham, Alabama, about forty miles south of the track. We all piled into our cars and raced down to the hospital.

He went into surgery as soon as he arrived. And finally, after what seemed like hours, the surgeon came out and said he was going to be all right.

After seeing the wreck over and over, to this day, it is difficult to understand how he could pull out of a wreck that bad with no more injuries than he had. He did suffer stress cracks to a couple of thoracic vertebrae. When the car flipped, the impact drove his head into his neck.

We prayed every moment for Ricky, along with millions of others. And we rejoice for his recovery. After a wreck like that, we all consider every day a bonus day.

I often ask, "What am I supposed to do now to repay for Ricky being spared?" That's a cross you can gladly bear, trying to discern what God wants you to do now. Ricky is very special to me. Who knows what's down the road for any of us?

DESIRÉ WILSON

Senior Pace Car Team
PPG Indy Car World Series

Few will argue that Desiré Wilson is the most versatile, experienced, and successful woman driver in history. And even the most ardent male chauvinist will have to admit that her career statistics rank up there with the most successful men as well.

It takes several pages just to list Desiré's significant accomplishments. She's raced more than eighty-three different cars in thirteen countries. She's enjoyed enviable success in Formula One, CART Indy Cars, WEC/GTP, Formula cars, Saloon cars, Trans-Ams, and virtually everything in between. She's won twenty-two races, set seventeen track records, and earned twelve poles.

The lady who was once named South African Sportswoman of the Year has cut back on her competitive racing in recent years—although she took time out in 1996 to place first overall and nab the pole position at the Detroit PPG Neon Challenge Race—to become one of the top spokespersons for PPG Industries and a much-in-demand radio and TV commentator.

I probably would have never gotten into car racing had it not been for my father. I was in a racing environment and started to race cars at age five. I went professional at the age of eighteen. My father worked on my race cars throughout my racing career. He was an exceptional mechanic, and while we didn't always have the finances it took to win every week, because of his exceptional ability, he always gave me an outstanding race car. As a result, we competed with the more expensive cars and big-bucks teams and won races.

After I had won the South African Formula 4 Championship, I met my husband, Alan. He said, "Let's go to Europe and see just how good you *really* are." We put all of our resources together, basically using money we earned in South Africa, to go to Europe, where we did pretty well. So, if it wasn't for my father and then Alan—we've now been married twenty-one years—I don't think I would have gotten as far as I did.

As a child, I remember praying to do well in my racing car. At that age, I think there was a belief in Jesus, but I'm not so sure that I really believed that He was my Savior. Even as a teenager, I'm not sure I really understood everything, but a belief in God and Jesus Christ was always there. Right through my life, I've always looked toward Jesus and believed in God and believed that there is some Greater Power that is guiding me and with me all the time.

I can't be specific as to a date, but I'd say around about 1985 or 1986, I was going through some traumatic times in my life because I was no longer racing Indy Cars and I *really* wanted to—and I wasn't really understanding what was happening to me. I don't think you realize how much you need the Lord until you lose things. All of a sudden I was thinking, *Why has this happened to me? Why am I not racing anymore? Why can't I find the financing? I want to drive race cars—and I can't!* I think I even went through a stage where I thought the Lord had abandoned me. At the time I thought, *I must have done something wrong. He's deserted me.*

That's when I met with Hunter Floyd of Motorsports Ministries and sat down and tried to understand what was happening to me. He made me understand that the Lord had *not* deserted me. He just wanted to change my way of life. It was time for a change. The Lord wanted me to go in a different direction. I saw that I should turn to the Lord and ask Him to help me that much more to get through the next stage in my life. It takes a while to try and understand and live with it, but I have in the last ten years.

Since then, I try to attend Hunter's church service every Sunday at the racetrack. The Motorsports Ministries services are a way of getting very close and keeping focused because it's difficult when you travel so much, and the Sundays when you could be in church, you're at the racetrack.

The driver is just a small point of the whole Indy Car situation. As we say, everybody is a team. But you're really a team only for that weekend. Once you get in an airplane on Sunday night, you're really not that much of a team anymore. You all go your separate ways and then you come together the next weekend. For this reason or some others, within the Indy Car circuit, everybody seems to be very private about religion.

I don't know what it is, but people are a little afraid of Christians, so they want to step away from you because they think that maybe you're going to be outspoken and try and talk to them about religion. People are just not very comfortable if they know that you're a Christian; therefore, it's hard to really go out and reach other people.

I make a statement every Sunday morning: "No, I can't do this interview right now. Is it possible for me to do it at a different time? I would like to go to church." So people realize that I go to church.

I work with PPG Industries now, and it's amazing how many people from there who are at the racetrack are now coming to the church services. Every week there are a couple more people who come. I think there are definitely people who look and sort of say, "Gee, if Desiré is going to admit that she's going to church, then I can."

I now wear a patch on my uniform that says "Motorsports Ministries." I'm not sure if people are avoiding me because of it. I think some people are not aware of what it means. Still, a lot of my friends and people I work with have started coming to church, people I never even knew had any interest in religion. Usually it's generated by something that's happened in their lives, or maybe when they see how I'm reacting to circumstances, how I may have changed over the years, they think, *Well, maybe this can help us.*

I don't normally open the discussion and ask people what their religion is or what their beliefs are, but if somebody talks to me and says, "I have a problem and I need somebody to talk with," I always say, "Please go and talk to Hunter because he really transformed my life. He helped me believe and understand how to accept and love the Lord."

Faith is extremely important when it comes to dangerous sports. But to be honest, you're driving a race car because it's what you dearly love to do and you have the God-given talent to do it. It's such an incredible challenge that you just want to go out there and be as successful as possible. My philosophy is, if I cannot be successful, there's no point in my doing it. I don't just want to drive around in the back of the field saying, "Gee, I'm having a good time driving a race car." Therefore, my commitment level is always what we call 110 percent in a race car. Your commitment is high, but so is the commitment in everybody around you.

Although we can say it's an extremely dangerous sport, relative to day-to-day life, it really isn't. Just about everybody on the racetrack knows what he or she is doing 99 percent of the time. Every now and again, we slip up. I truly believe that you have to have that faith in yourself and everybody around you, but also that inner faith. You must believe that Somebody is there with you all the time.

I'm not saying I have often avoided accidents or that they have been minuscule because of my faith. But I truly believe my faith saved my life one day at Le Mans where I was doing 220 mph and all of a sudden I was feeling that the car just wasn't quite right. I had to make a split-second decision. *Do I do one more lap? Or do I pit right this instant?* I made the decision to head for the pits. The crew didn't find the problem, so out I went again. Suddenly, I had an accident within one hundred yards of the pits—but at a much lower speed, going maybe eighty miles per hour as opposed to 220 miles per hour. Getting out of the car, I said to myself, "There was definitely Somebody here. The Lord was with me all the way."

You might ask, "Why would the Lord make those decisions for you?" I truly believe that while it may have been my reaction, at the same time there was Somebody there telling me what to do. That's probably the first time I got out of a race car and said, "Thank You, Lord," knowing that He saved my life. I used to think it was luck, but now I believe it's a direction.

Memorable Moment

I have to say there are probably two races, two totally different types of races, that come to mind. One was winning the British Formula 1 Championship race in England. That was really just so incredible for me because I had some adversity just before it. I did say a little prayer just before the race started. Then I said, "If I lead into the first turn, I'm going to win this race." I got into the first turn first, led the race, and then there was an accident, so we had to have a restart. That was even more traumatic for me because I had to do this all over again. I said, "Dear Lord, just be with me. If I lead into the first turn, then I'm going to win." Just being so focused, I got into the first turn first *again* and won the race. That's a great memory for me.

Then I had another race, the World Championship race in Italy, which was a little bit different in that while I was leading, it started raining. I had to slow down because we didn't have time to do a pit stop to change tires and the second-position car was catching me. I had to let him by, and basically either finish second or crash. I made the decision to let him pass because we needed the points, we needed the finish. Suddenly, the car that overtook me made an error, and I won the race by just seconds. That was almost a greater achievement because it was one of those races where I'd almost lost.

JEFF HAMMOND

Team Manager
#17
Western Auto's Parts America
Darrell Waltrip Motorsports Chevrolet Monte
Carlo

Jeff Hammond has been with Darrell Waltrip an amazing fifteen years in a sport where the annual "Silly Season" sees a quarter of the players change partners. Once touted as the calming influence to Darrell's noted fiery competitive nature, Jeff and Darrell are now more like partners, equal pieces of the racing puzzle.

Before joining Darrell, Jeff worked with a host of famous and not-so-famous teams and drivers. But he'll always be best known as the voice on the radio that talked Darrell through the final laps of the heart-stopping Daytona 500, coasting on fumes, drafts, and an unshaken trust in God.

I was raised in Charlotte, North Carolina, in a Methodist home. We did the usual things, going to church every Sunday. Mom, my grandmother, and my family were very big supporters of the church locally. So I spent a lot of time with a lot of people who really lived a Christian life on a regular basis. It was almost like living with preachers.

When I was growing up, I spent a lot of time working with

the youth. In our church we especially had several youth Sundays during the summer.

But if I were to say what really had brought me to a closer understanding and appreciation of what Jesus can do and what God really means to me in my life, I'd have to say it was a couple of things.

First, it has been through a lot of tragedies, seeing things that a lot of individuals don't see and hopefully don't get a chance to see. At the same time, tragedies give you an understanding of how fragile life is and an appreciation about having somebody to talk to. I mean, you can talk to your wife, you can talk to your father, you can talk to your mother. But I don't feel the same kind of comfort. I think that's where I feel the biggest difference.

When I was growing up I worked in a rescue squad. I've had a lot of friends who have gotten killed or hurt in racing. You keep asking yourself the question, *Why does this go on? Why does this have to be that way? Can this be fair?* Whenever I question it, I think about a lot of the things I've heard and learned when I was growing up with the Bible and the teachings of the many pastors that I've listened to. They taught me it's not our place to question. It's not our place to try to reason some of the things that come about. Instead, I need to know that those things happen because it's God's will and they're all for a purpose. They happen to give you a better understanding of how to appreciate what you do have and how fragile what you have is.

Still, seeing these tragedies and sometimes trying to look by them and carry on, it's real easy to want to crawl back into a shell and try to live a real, real sheltered life. We think, *Well, if I don't do anything to run a risk of getting hurt, or if I don't do anything to expose myself or my feelings, then I'll never have to deal with these things.*

But I think I've become stronger because of it. This is probably one of the lamest reasons that you could ever give anybody during the time of a tragedy, that "this was God's will." But if you believe that, you can find that comfort and understanding.

Today's society is so much more fragile than it's ever been. When I do things wrong, that's when I feel the worst because I want to do right. I know He knows that when I do wrong the guilt is just overwhelming. But the feeling that comes when you get back to where you should be, there's *nothing* that feels any better . . .

except maybe being around people who understand and realize that you're going to make mistakes. Once you understand that there is forgiveness, that there is salvation, and there is a purpose for your life, it's a lot easier to go on.

The second thing that brought me to an understanding of Jesus as a personal Savior was my wife, Sharon. Motorsports took me away from my church. But when I got married, Sharon was a Baptist and she had her local church. That's where I started attending shortly after we got married.

Since then, I've really enjoyed the time that I do get to spend at home and at church. There are some really great people there. It's like the church I grew up in; it's very neighborhood-based. There are a lot of people there who have a lot of energy, and it's nice to be around them.

And when I'm gone for long periods of time, it's like coming home. Everybody's really, really nice. They genuinely make me feel that they're glad to see me. After all, there are times where I'll go eleven or twelve Sundays before I get a chance to go back to church. Even so, when I go in, I don't feel that they're thinking, *Well, what's he showing up for? He doesn't belong here.* You get the feeling that they've missed you.

Another thing is, they keep up with what you're doing and understand some of the ups and downs you've been going through. So that's the nice part about belonging to, what I consider, a really good church.

It's tough to be involved in this sport and to be able to give the time back that you should to the church and to God. There's not a day goes by that you don't wish there was some way you could change some of the things you're doing so you could spend a little more time in those relationships. I find that many times I go to church and end up envious of people who have the opportunity to be more involved in church-related situations.

Thank God there is Max Helton at the racetrack. Sometimes we get so carried away, we get so involved, we don't have a lot of time to go to services. Fortunately, he's the kind of individual who never lets you feel as if you're totally lost. He's always coming by with a good word and a prayer. I think that's the one thing that probably makes it bearable for a lot of us. We realize that we don't live the lives that we really need to. He keeps reminding us that we need to at least try.

Memorable Moment

It's so hard to pick just one event as the most memorable. I don't think there's a race that goes by that you don't ask God to help you get through it. Also, I ask Him to help us win every time. When we're getting real, real close to winning it, I talk to Him continuously, every lap, whispering, "Please, Lord, don't let us down now. We're too close here; just don't let us down. Don't let us make the wrong decision here."

Maybe I'm asking for the wrong thing. But it's always nice that you *can* ask and feel that maybe it's not too far out of line.

Having said all of that, probably the one race that really sticks out the most would be Daytona in 1989. Darrell Waltrip had always wanted to win that race. We came close several times and had some really good runs. It was neat the way it came down because it was the seventeenth try and car #17—on February 17!

We were running well, but we wound up having to use a little bit of strategy and say a lot of prayers to try to make sure that his car didn't run out of gas. We wound up winning the race because of the gas mileage. The last two or three laps, Darrell was hollering at me on the radio, "I'm out of gas!" and I'm shouting back, "No, man, you just keep shaking, it's running, you just keep going!"

Somebody else helped us get through that day. It was very memorable because of the excitement and the joy it brought Darrell, fulfilling a lifelong desire to win a race that everybody wants to win. I was real, real lucky to be a part of that.

Of course, just being around Darrell and his wife, Stevie, and always believing that good things can happen to those who believe has been great. Watching Darrell evolve and grow in his Christian life has been a nice experience.

Right now, a lot of good things aren't really happening around our shop, but we keep believing that sooner or later we'll get over the top. And when we do, this will be a thing of the past and we won't worry about it. I kept telling Darrell and Stevie, during the time they were trying to have their first child, "Just have the faith." And now they've got Jessica and they've got Sarah, so miracles do happen to people who believe.

DON MEREDITH

Vice President, Joe Gibbs Racing
#18
Interstate Batteries Racing
Joe Gibbs Racing Chevrolet Monte Carlo

In a world filled with contradictions, Don Meredith (no relation to the former football great) sees nothing incompatible in pairing a family-oriented ministry with high-performance stock cars. That's because Meredith is affiliated with one of the most faith-driven racing teams in the world. From chief sponsor Norm Miller to owner Joe Gibbs to crew chief Jimmy Makar, many members of the car crew and office staff of the fluorescent, lime-colored #18 team are outspoken about their religious faith.

And in the heady atmosphere of high-performance gasoline fumes and crowds of 300,000 howling in unison, Don provides a calming presence amid the chaos, always gently reminding one and all of life's true destination, one that's far beyond the checkered flags of this world.

My grandmother was a Christian, but my parents were not religious at all. My grandmother was an ordained minister and, from my earliest moments, she shared Christ with me. I actually received Christ at a Billy Graham Crusade at the Rice University stadium in Houston, Texas, in the early 1950s. I didn't really get serious, though, until Campus Crusade came along because I'd never gotten the full picture that the Christian life was a moment-by-moment thing. I knew clearly that I'd received Christ, but I didn't know the rest of it.

In college I began to encounter my first real tests in life, mainly losing the love of my high school sweetheart. That put me in a tailspin. Then I began to have some struggles in my studies. For the first time, I began to realize that I wasn't necessarily going to be successful in life.

Right at that particular time, I ran into a really neat guy with Campus Crusade, and, boy, I got excited about a moment-by-moment Christian life.

I've had four or five really serious, coming-to-the-end type of experiences over the years, and each one of those deepened my dependence. The Christian life kind of comes in waves. I tend to hit highs, then the Lord will bring me low. At fifty-five, you look forward to enjoying those high ones and yet when you look back at the low ones, they're probably the most meaningful in your life in the long run.

When Joe Gibbs and I began to work together, probably thirteen years ago, that partnership eventually led to the racing team. But I actually have a ministry of my own called Christian Family Life. It is a ministry we started twenty-five years ago after getting married and realizing that I had some real needs in that area. My wife, Sally, and I began to search the Scriptures, and our lives were revolutionized by what we found. So we started Christian Family Life, and it's really been my vocation over the years. For many years, we did seminars all over the country. Then Sally and I helped start the family ministry of Campus Crusade for Christ. They credit Sally and me with much of the material they use since it was originally ours.

Dennis Rainey became involved at the University of Arkansas when we were on Crusade staff together. When we started Christian Family Life, we recruited Dennis from their ministry to high school students. He's the head of Christian Family Life now. He became the director when I moved to Washington, D.C. That's where I met Joe.

When Joe's career ended in football, he said that he'd really like to try racing. So five years ago he and I came down to Charlotte and actually threw a fleece out to the Lord and made some significant contacts, mainly Norm and Tommy Miller of Interstate Batteries, two really committed Christian men. The Lord led us to share Joe's dream with them and about a week later, Norm and Tommy made a commitment to become our first sponsors. The next thing you knew, we were in racing!

We were able to get Dale Jarrett and Jimmy Makar to help us put the team together, and it just began to roll from there. Then a little over two years ago, both Joe and I moved to Charlotte.

The Gibbs family owns the race team 100 percent, but we're spiritual partners. I work with them. He's offered me ownership, but I have not accepted because my commitment is to be an encouragement to the Gibbs family. At the same time, he helps me in my ministry.

I stay focused on Christian Family Life as a really key element, but I spend about forty hours a week in racing and about forty hours in ministry in marriage. So we're kind of a unique combination. So much of racing is on the weekend that it leaves the weekdays free.

My wife and I have now taken the marriage materials from the Christian Family Life ministry and put them in a twelve-week home-study series, and we're distributing that nationally. Six couples at a time can go through the material in the study book. We're in eleven or so states right now. As we travel around the country, we time our visits with the races. The material is set up in a way that is very easy to lead people through; we just help train couples to feel the confidence to do that.

Sally and I recently got back from three races in Denver, Seattle, and San Francisco. We spent two or three days at each one of those races and between them, we trained couples on how to teach the study. For instance, on the way up to Seattle, we stopped in Oregon and trained some couples there. So we try to mix all of that together.

Joe has a strong commitment to help me with that, and I help him with the other. So it works out that we go seven days a week. My kids are grown and Sally is very involved, helping with the racing as well as Christian Family Life, so we go together. It has been a real joy for us.

Memorable Moment

In terms of a highlight in racing, our very first race during our second year as a team, we were able to win the Daytona 500. That's certainly been the highlight to this point because Joe had won Super Bowls in football. Just to watch him and his family and to see their encouragement was a joy for us.

The overwhelming thing that hits you in racing is how hard it is to win a race. The first year when we ran Daytona, our very first race, we started thirty-eighth and finished seventh. We thought, *Gee, this racing is easy!* Dale Jarrett was driving for us back then. And then all of a sudden we had a massive wreck and just destroyed the car. That was a reality point for us. After that, we didn't do all that well our first year.

So to come into the second year and go to Daytona and to get to the end of the race and actually see Dale move up those last two slots near the front with both of our families right there in the pits—it was exhilarating! Then to pass on that last lap and to be in front of Dale Earnhardt and for Dale Jarrett to ultimately win, well, that was just magnificent!

JOHNNY PARSONS, JR.

1996 Indy 500 ride
Team Blueprint Racing, Inc. 1993 Lola

Johnny Parsons is the middle name in a racing dynasty. He's son of the late Johnnie Woodrow Parsons (1949 national champion and 1950 Indy winner) and the father of Johnny Parsons III (a popular young racer with his own home page on the World Wide Web).

But Parsons is no Johnny-come-lately to racing. He started racing Quarter-Midgets at age twelve, moved to go-Karts at age sixteen, and advanced to three-quarter and full-sized Midgets at age eighteen. He passed his driver's test at Indy in 1973 and has been racing successfully in every major sanctioned division ever since. In fact, one week after the 1996 Indianapolis 500, he finished third in the Copper World Classic at Phoenix in the Midget division!

Actually, Johnny's return to the Brickyard in 1996 after an absence of ten years was one of the great stories coming out of Indianapolis in May. And while his finish (suspension problems after starting sixteenth) didn't match his fifth-place finishes of 1977 and 1985, it proved once again that there's plenty of life in this middle man yet!

I didn't come from a Christian family, but there was a seed planted when I was seven years old. Since my parents were on the racing circuit, I got passed around a lot from ages about one to eight. I lived with an aunt for a while and went to Sunday school with her. Sunday school planted the seed that there was a God. After that, though, I never really attended much church.

Years later, when I got married, we wanted to get married in a church. The church we chose required that we attend there *and* attend some marital counseling sessions, so we did. And that planted more seeds. But it wasn't until later in my life—it seems that it took me forty years to grow up—that it "took."

A need began to grow in my life, particularly when I was down in the dumps, not knowing where I was going with my life. I experienced problems with sexual immorality and got a divorce. I lived with several women over the next few years, and my house was a continual party. This was about 1984.

I didn't know it at the time, but a couple of runaways began staying at my apartment when I was out of town. When I came back from a racing trip, the gals were still there—and so was the sheriff! I didn't know they were runaways *or* underage! When I watched the evening news a couple of nights later, I saw that I was accused of harboring juveniles. My own kids were in junior high and high school and they were humiliated. It was a major embarrassment.

Sometimes it takes being rocked that hard before people like me will listen. I was almost to the point of suicide before it was all settled. With my career just about over, I tried, but I couldn't find any kind of satisfaction from any other type of employment. As far as personal happiness, I was chasing the wind. (In my later walk, Ecclesiastes has given me a lot to relate to!) When you've been shaken as I was, sometimes you take a step back and look at things. I did, and I saw a life that was out of control. I was headed for destruction. And it scared me. Finally, one day I dropped to my knees. I gave up. I admitted I couldn't control my life. I couldn't control myself. I couldn't handle it. I asked for help. I got some counseling, psychiatric as well as religious.

Then I drew on those seeds that had been planted in my life years ago and went to the Scriptures. I began to pray about what to do. The next thing I did was join a Bible study. And through all of that, the Lord blessed me and brought me to a personal walk with Him.

The girl I was dating at the time, Kitty, had suffered through some of this with me, but stood by me. We got married in 1992, and I've been active in my church ever since.

With all of the bad publicity, I never thought I'd get another ride at Indy. In the late '80s and early '90s, I drove a few cars, but none of them were competitive.

One of the basic Scriptures that people go to is Proverbs 3:5: "Trust in the LORD with all your heart, / And lean not on your own understanding." I wasn't sure if I was meant to be back in racing. I gave up on it; I didn't think I'd ever get to return.

But during the month of May, when practice and qualifying were going on, I was over at the Speedway and a guy came up to me and said, "We need you to put the car in the race."

I said, "I'll get back to you tomorrow. I need to pray about this."

I did—and I realized that the Lord wanted me to be in racing to show the miracles He can perform in individuals. He turned my life around in front of everybody.

It was about this time that I met Hunter Floyd and Motorsports Ministries. Since then, the Lord's used me in any way He wants to. I frequently go back to Proverbs 3:5 when I'm wondering, *What's He going to do with me now—and how's He going to do it?*

I had to get broken down before I could return to racing. I was too filled with pride before, which is what happens to people who think they're in control and have all of the power.

After returning to Indy, I told a number of interviewers: "The most important thing to me right now is not what I thought it was. It's what people take for granted: your faith, your family, your kids, your grandkids. If you put things in their proper perspective, it is a step in the right direction."

Memorable Moment

It was the first time I qualified for the Indy 500. I moved to Indiana when I was about eight and stayed all through junior high school and high school. Then I moved to California to start a racing career. I grew up at the track, around the cars and stars. I wanted to be like them. Watching it early on, I took on some role models that were undesirable. That helped lead me the way I chose to go. My father wasn't around much. My parents divorced young, and my stepfather was always gone to racetracks and garages. So I picked up some bad habits along the way.

The first time I got on the track to take my rookie test was a big deal. Then qualifying for my first race there was another big highlight. Since then, there have been other racing achievements, winning some races and qualifying again for the 1996 Indy 500.

I'd have to say another highlight has just been spending time with my grandkids. Kids are great. I had a lot of fun with my sons, but I don't understand how come grandkids are so much more fun! They'll bring you close to the Lord. I enjoy every moment I spend with them. I know that sounds old-fashioned, but that's the way I prefer to be.

There have been other, not-so-good memorable moments, of course. I was involved in an accident in the summer of 1996 in Richmond, Virginia, in a Midget car. My head hit the wall and my helmet broke. I was unconscious for ten or fifteen minutes and dizzy for a couple of days. Looking at the helmet and tape of the accident later, I realized that accident should have caused injuries leading to coma if not death—certainly permanent head injuries. So I get reaffirmed regularly that I'm still around here for a reason.

You get a close call like that and you're in praise for quite some time afterward, even for the simple daily things in life. God's protecting us, and it's all for a reason. We've just got to remain humble and give all credit where it is due.

The Lord has put in me a great love for His Word. I need it. I need daily fellowship with others. I often stop during the day to try and figure out what the Lord's plan for me is. We have the annual meeting with Motor Racing Outreach, there's fellowship with Christians in Bible studies, and there are my own private morning devotions and Scripture readings. All of that definitely helps.

That's the key—it has to be a daily walk. When I look at the scary side of how I used to be, I definitely don't want to go back.

CLIFF CHAMPION

Shop Foreman
#41
Larry Hedrick Motorsports
Kodiak Racing Monte Carlo

Cliff Champion is a tall, lanky, bubbling mass of contradictions. Seemingly easygoing and affable on the surface, he's a noted perfectionist. Content as shop foreman for the famed #41 Kodiak Racing/Larry Hedrick Motorsports team, he's been a top crew chief with a number of feared teams. He was even one of the few crew members interviewed in-depth in Peter Golenbock's book, American Zoom.

Cliff is unusually open and vulnerable in a day when most people calculate each word. He'll tell you how to break down Ricky Craven's brawny Monte Carlo in the same infinite detail as he'll discuss his tumultuous life.

Perhaps that's because after years of rushing headlong into life, Cliff Champion has found the peace that only Jesus Christ can bring. And if you give him a minute, he'll gladly tell you about it.

I didn't come from what I would call a real Christian family. I came to Jesus probably like a lot of people: I didn't know anything about it, I ignored it, and then I hit on some hardships and found the need.

I had a little bit of church when I was a real small kid. My mom took me to Sunday school, but my dad owned his own business and worked day and night.

When I was about twenty-one, I went to a big church for a while in Virginia Beach, Virginia. But I didn't get anything out of it. I was going through the motions. I heard the preacher, but it was as if he was speaking in a foreign tongue. It didn't mean a thing to me—I just went because I thought it was neat to go to church. I finally quit going.

Racing was all that I knew. You have to have some kind of confidence in your life, and that's where I got it.

I'd been racing ten or fifteen years when I married. I'd had girlfriends who came and went, but no one meant anything. Just the racing—it was always going to be there. When I met this one girl, I found that there were things in life besides racing. She fulfilled the other needs in life I had.

After we'd been married for four years, I wanted to get out of racing because it takes so much of your time. I wanted to be able to take my kids camping or fishing or go to a ball game with them. Racing doesn't allow that. We didn't have any kids yet, but I wanted to build for the future.

So I left racing and started a business. Any time you start a business, money gets tight. When it did I didn't realize how much it bothered my wife. The intimacy was missing from our marriage. After a couple of months, it was completely gone.

Finally, in late October of '92, I asked her one night, "What's wrong?"

She said, "I'm leaving."

I realized right then that she meant everything to me. There was nobody else I had even considered quitting racing for.

I couldn't handle it. I even tried to commit suicide several times in the months that followed.

In January, I went to work for Phil Parsons and the very first day I told him, "I need help. I can't handle this. I'm not the smartest guy in the world, but I'm not the stupidest, either. Three times I've tried to kill myself. I am not so stupid that, sooner or later, I won't get it right."

He said, "I know just the person you need to talk to." Phil put me in touch with Max Helton right away. I'd seen the chapel services at the racetrack, but I never had time for them. I was always too busy. But that very Monday morning I went down and talked to Max and he didn't give me the hard sell or anything. He just tried to comfort me a little bit. He could tell I didn't really know anything about God.

MRO was having their yearly conference that weekend in Hilton Head, South Carolina, so he said, "Why don't you come? It'll do you some good." I went down.

There probably wasn't a specific speaker that changed things for me. A lot of churches you go to, the teaching is straight out of the Bible, with all of these "thees" and "thous" and it is like listening to Shakespeare. But the speakers at this conference spoke to me in everyday language. I heard the Word of God for the first time. When they talked, it was as though they were talking to me, and it was exactly what I needed to hear.

I listened to the speakers all that first day and we'd just finished up about eight that night. While we were sitting around talking afterward, I kept saying over and over, "This is great! How great it is to hear the Word of God!" Then Max explained the Sinner's Prayer to me. When he was through, he said, "Would you like to pray that prayer?" Right then I said, "Yes!" I accepted Christ that Friday night.

To be nowhere with Christ before and all of a sudden to be at the top, I felt this was a whole new deal. I went to every class they had on Saturday. They spent a lot of time telling us how to give our testimony. Then they wanted to practice giving our testimony in about three minutes on a partner. A girl and I started practicing our testimonies and, after a few moments, she began crying. When time was up, they gave me another partner and when I told him my testimony, *he* began crying.

That night a bunch of us got in the hot tub and I ended up next to singer Susie Luchsinger, Reba McEntire's sister, who sang at the program earlier. Her husband was my *third* partner and he urged me to tell my testimony to Susie. I did and all of them began crying, right there in the hot tub!

Sunday we went on this outreach program with MRO to the nearby Paris Island marine base. I was a last–minute addition to the conference, and I ended up at the artillery range. Once there, they said, "We need somebody to speak, to say a few words, and the rest of you will hand out these little pamphlets."

And me, being saved for all of two days now, said, "Pal, I'm the best little pamphlet hander-outer you've ever seen—you give them to me!"

Lake Speed was there and he was asked to speak; Lake's a real strong Christian. As we waited for the building to be unlocked, I saw all of these young, bald-headed recruits coming up. While they were standing there, I was thinking, *Maybe what I've been through will mean something to these kids.* Their chaplain was with us and I went up to him and said, "Could I say something?" I got up there and gave my testimony for the first time. It took about twenty minutes.

At the end, I said, "As racers, we have to see something to believe it. Somebody tells you, 'Put this spoiler on your car and you'll pick up a half-second,' and we'll say, 'Well, we'll try it.' But we don't automatically put it on and go.

"I haven't seen God, I haven't seen Jesus Christ. But I can tell you I *know* what He's done in my life in three days—that's good enough for me."

When I got down, I saw Lake was crying! It was his turn to speak and he said, "I know Cliff, but I've never heard his testimony before. I'm supposed to speak, but I can't touch this."

It was an amazing transformation in those three days!

Memorable Moment

I can't really think of just one. It's all been good. Probably winning your first race is always special. I was working with Buddy Baker and this was the first real big team that I ever worked for. The first race we went to as a team was Daytona—and we won the 500 in 1983!

We won the Pit Crew Championship with Benny Parsons as the driver a year later. I was crew chief at the time.

Another year, we won the pole at Charlotte with Benny. We ended up winning two or three races together.

Ricky Rudd and I grew up together, we lived about two blocks from each other. So we started out racing together right there. He was the driver for the old Gatorade team years ago and we got him his first pole. We got two poles that year.

Then I went to work for Alan Kulwicki in 1987 and got him his first pole at Richmond.

You feel good whenever that happens, but you always know it was a team effort. It's never you. You're just glad to be a part of it.

DAVID SMITH

Crew Chief
#3
Richard Childress Racing
GM Goodwrench Service Chevrolet Monte Carlo

Dale Earnhardt's fearsome reputation as "The Intimidator" owes as much to the appearance of the menacing black #3 and his legendary pit crews as it does to Dale's pedal-to-the-metal style of driving. David Smith (no relation to Marcus), is the latest in a long line of winning crew chiefs with the Richard Childress Racing team.

Interestingly enough, David worked his way through the ranks at RCR, first as a jack man (winning Skoal All-Pro recognition six times), and now as chief of one of NASCAR's most celebrated and successful teams. David's team invariably ensures that Dale is one of the first cars back on the track after each frenzied pit stop.

So while steely-eyed Dale continues his unbroken string of successes on the tracks, it is David who calls the shots on pit row.

I was brought up in a religious home. We went to church, but it wasn't a real strong gospel-preaching church. Dad would get us up on Sunday morning, and we knew we were going to church because that was the right thing to do. He was brought up that way.

By the time I got to be fourteen or fifteen, I became rebellious and quit going to church. My dad couldn't do much with me; I basically just took off on my own. This was during the sixties, so I got into the world real good. I became a hippie, doing drugs and alcohol and the whole deal. I turned completely against God and anything to do with God.

But some men whom my dad worked with and who knew the Lord witnessed to him at work, and he ended up getting saved. After that, he started going to a different church, one that was more gospel-centered. Then he started working on me! I was about nineteen or twenty at the time. He started giving me Scriptures from the Bible about what salvation was and how we were all sinners and needed Jesus Christ.

I'd say, "Dad, when I get old like you, I'll get religion then." I was pretty sarcastic in those days.

But he always reminded me, "What if you die today? What if you go to one of these parties tonight and you get shot? What if you wreck your car and die? Where do you think you'll be?"

I said, "Well, I guess I'll be out there pushing up daisies!"

He said, "No. You've got a soul. That soul is either going to spend eternity in heaven with the Lord or spend eternity in hell in damnation and punishment."

Of course, I didn't want to hear all of *that!* I just kept living my life, getting involved in the party scene. I continued this way until I was twenty-five years old.

On my twenty-fifth birthday, my mother gave me a Bible. We were brought up with Bibles in our home; I just never took the time to read them. I'd heard all the stories in it, but I never considered *who* Jesus Christ or God really was. When my mother gave me that Bible, I just thanked her for it, took it home, put it in a drawer, and promptly forgot about it.

I was a real popular person, I had plenty of girlfriends and lived that party lifestyle. But one day when I came home from work, I finally realized that things just weren't fun anymore. I was drinking a lot, I was smoking a lot of dope, I was taking a lot of pills, but nothing seemed to be fun.

Something impressed me to go get that Bible out of my drawer. I sat down and just started reading it. Even so, I argued with myself the whole way: *What are you doing? You've never had a desire to do this before. Why are you doing it now?*

My mother had underlined a bunch of key Scriptures. One of

the first ones I found, of course, was John 3:16: "For God so loved the world that He gave His only begotten Son, that whoever believes in Him should not perish but have everlasting life."

I'd paid enough attention in school to know that that "whoever" included me. As I kept reading, I found other Scriptures, such as Romans 3:23, "For all have sinned and fall short of the glory of God," and Romans 6:23, "For the wages of sin is death, but the gift of God is eternal Life in Christ Jesus our Lord." And other ones, such as Romans 10:9, "If you confess with your mouth the Lord Jesus and believe in your heart that God has raised Him from the dead, you will be saved," and Romans 10:13, "For 'whoever calls on the name of the LORD shall be saved.'"

I sat there and read that Bible for a couple of hours, perhaps even more. I was high at the time because I'd been drinking some and had smoked a joint. But I kept reading, and I became so engrossed in what it was saying that I realized it was speaking *to me*. This Word that I was holding in my hands, this Book was actually speaking to me and telling me where I was!

I couldn't go to sleep that night. I tried to close my eyes and I couldn't. I was afraid that I wouldn't wake up. I tossed and turned and got up and down all night long just thinking about what I'd read. I couldn't get the Lord out of my mind. I couldn't get God out of my mind. I couldn't get how I'd lived and rejected God out of my mind.

I called my mother real early the next morning, a few days before Christmas in 1975. She knew something was wrong for me to call that early—like 6:30 in the morning!

She said, "Are you okay?"

I said, "I don't know. Things just aren't right. Nothing's really fun anymore." I'd always been an upbeat person, a happy-type person, even though I was living in sin. No longer. I finally told her, "Momma, I've been up all night reading that Bible you gave me. I just couldn't go to sleep. This thing has really got my mind turned around, just thinking about all of this."

I could tell that she was crying.

I said, "Mom, are *you* okay?"

She said, "I'm fine, but I couldn't sleep any at all last night, either! At about 10:30, the Lord so burdened me about you that I've been up all night praying for you on my knees."

So God was really at work in that.

I went on into work the next few days, then on Christmas we went up to my grandmother's where we always had a big dinner together.

Dad asked the blessing before we ate. He thanked God for everybody's health, the blessings of the year, the usual things. But the last thing he said, and I think he knew that the Lord was really dealing with me then, was, "Lord, if there is anybody here in our family who doesn't know You, and doesn't know Jesus Christ as his Savior, we just pray that You'd save him today."

It hit me right in the heart! I mean, it just really hit me hard. I went running out of the old farmhouse and ended up out by the barn. I looked up at heaven and said, "God, I give up. I know I'm a sinner and I know that I'm going to hell if I don't get to know You. I don't want to go to hell. I believe that Jesus Christ died for me, just as Momma's Bible said. I believe what You said in Your Word and I want Jesus Christ to come into my heart."

And He did. Right there, right then, right on that farm.

The Lord came into my heart and I knew at that moment that all of the guilt was gone, the burden was lifted off my shoulders. I'd felt so guilty all that week after reading the Bible. In its place a joy and a warmness and a complete peace came into my life. *Right then*.

I stayed out there thirty or forty minutes, just kind of laughing and crying and thanking the Lord for what He did for me.

And I made Him a promise. I said, "Lord, I realize who You are now. And I realize how much You love me even while I rejected You, even while I was living such a sinful life, even though I cursed Your name and hated the people that I chanced upon in the street who tried to give me gospel tracts. So, the best I can, I'll serve You. You take my life and You use it for Your glory. Because I've failed trying to lead my own life."

And that's what He's done.

Memorable Moment

Several stand out. Our first Winston Cup Championship in 1986 with Richard Childress and Dale Earnhardt is still very big in my mind. I had been with Richard Childress since 1979, when Richard was still driving. I was here when Earnhardt came the first time, and I was here when he came back in 1984. I've been here for all of the championships.

In 1987 in Charlotte, Earnhardt became famous for what they now call "the pass in the grass"—that always stands out as a real big win. Bill Elliott had everybody smoked that day, but Dale just kind of outdrove him and outfoxed him and ended up winning that race.

Then the 1995 Brickyard—that was tremendous. In front of 300,000-plus people, just the magnitude and the history of that track make it something. Our pit crew, the last pit stop we made, actually put Dale out front. So that was a real big event, and stands out in my mind as well.

TODD FIELDS

Spotter/Engineer
#88
Ford Quality Care
Robert Yates Racing Ford Thunderbird

On race day, Todd Fields has a job like few others in NASCAR racing. He sits high above the action, like the offensive and defensive coaches in football, watching the entire race, maintaining continual radio contact with his driver, Dale Jarrett. Todd is Dale's eye in the sky.

(Actually, on the days before the races, Todd has an even higher viewpoint—he's the team pilot as well. But that's another story.)

"Basically, the spotter's job is to help the driver throughout the race," Todd says. "One, letting him know where wrecks are. And two, keeping him calm. It's hard for a real competitor to do this, but Dale trusts me. I'll say, 'Dale, let this guy by you.' I'll do that because the guy is racing him so hard, he's liable to wreck. So I say, 'Hey, let him by. We'll get him later on down the road.' And Dale believes me."

And that's not a bad analogy for the Christian faith. Only God has the big picture for our lives. We just need to trust Him and let Him lead.

Frrom day one, from birth, I grew up in the church and in a church family. My mom had a degree in

Christian education from Nyack University in New York. My sister currently attends Wheaton College, and she's interested in Christian education. That's always been behind us throughout my entire life. I can't remember a Sunday not getting up and going to church.

It was 1978, I believe, that I made a public profession of faith. I was about twelve. It seems that the people I'm talking to, the specific date is more instrumental. Whenever they accepted Christ seems to be more of a moment. Obviously, growing up in a church family, we had always talked about it. But it wasn't like the accounts of some you hear. I do remember living in Ohio at the time when it happened. I remember that Friday night or whatever when we all sat down and talked about it. But it wasn't one of those life-changing stories that a lot of people have.

This profession, like any professional sport, probably tests your faith more than anything out there. First, because of the temptations that are out there—and there are maybe even more in this sport than most professional sports. Second, because you're always gone on Sundays.

Take this past Sunday. We got in from Indy early Sunday morning. Then to try to get up and say, "Well, okay, it's Sunday." It's hard, not having been in your regular church for eight or nine weeks, to drag yourself out of bed and do it. It's just hard. More so even for me, being my age of twenty-seven, the pressures that I see from all the other crew guys, the people that I see not walking a Christian path. It's kind of like you're a black sheep because you might not go out and do a lot of the things that everybody else does. You know that it's not right to do them, but everybody else is. You just have to stand your ground.

Most of our faith-building is done during the week and in private devotions. For our part, as far as the racers go, the biggest thing that has come our way is the Motor Racing Outreach. Without that, none of us would have a place to go worship on Sunday mornings. That's such a great fellowship.

Even so, a lot of times the crew guys have a hard time making it because it depends on if the car is through with specs or not. Some Sundays you make it, some you don't. But to know that it is always there, that is neat.

We also have a Bible study here at our shop. At least once a month, Max Helton comes in and leads a Bible study. We have about eight to twelve guys. Robert Yates's dad was a Baptist minister, his brothers and sisters are missionaries. So Robert and his brother Richard come from a Christian family. You can see that intertwined within this organization, that they do try to really focus on the families. You work seventy, eighty hours a week, but they do try to include your family whenever they can. You can even tell by the way Robert acts and the way they do things that they respect you and your feelings. In the team meeting, the last thing we do is recite the Lord's Prayer—little things like that.

It's not a lot, but most of us can't take hours out of the day to have a long devotion or Bible study, so we try to do something along the way.

Memorable Moment

It would have to be August 3, 1996, at the Brickyard 400 at Indy.

I grew up in Carmel, Indiana. I remember my dad taking me to the Indianapolis 500 when I was twelve. Dad gave me a clipboard and an umbrella, and I snuck my way into the garage area. Growing up on the Indy Car side and watching those people on Victory Lane—that track has a lot more meaning for me. For a lot of the guys on the NASCAR side, Daytona is their big track. That's where they grew up, always going to races. But for me, having grown up in Indy, to have won a Brickyard 400 and been able to stand in Victory Lane there—now *that* was something. That was probably the highlight of my life.

Throughout all the races, my viewpoint is a lot different from the guys in the pits because I'm the spotter. It's kind of like when God is up high above you, watching over you. He knows what's going to happen down the road. He has the big picture.

The guys in the pits, the only thing they see is what's right in front of them. They don't know what's happening in turn one or turn two or three or four, they just see that car go right by them. But being up there and being able to watch Dale around the entire racetrack, it's a different feeling. You get more involved in the race and are really watching. You develop more understanding of how your driver is driving and watch him as the race develops, particularly as he's coming up through the pack.

There at Indy in 1996, it was Dale and Ernie racing side by side. This was not racing for a win at Martinsville. This was racing for one of the biggest races that we do.

At the end there was a caution with about two laps to go and I remember shouting to Dale, "Come on, Dale, race for the flag! Go, go, go, go!" Because I knew if he got the caution flag, we had it. To see Dale come and take the lead, it was just unbelievable.

BOBBY HILLIN

Driver/Owner
#77
Jasper Engines/Federal Mogul
Jasper Motorsports Ford Thunderbird

Bobby Hillin's lean, rock-hard frame is crisscrossed with scars, the trophies of a no-holds-barred attitude in life's school of hard knocks. Sound melodramatic? Consider this brief biography. He:

- had several near-death experiences as a child.
- began driving mini-stocks at Abilene (Texas) Speedway at age thirteen.
- passed up a football scholarship to make his NASCAR Winston Cup debut at age seventeen at North Wilkesboro in 1982.
- became, at age twenty-two years, one month, and twenty-two days, the youngest driver to ever win a superspeedway race, the 1986 Talladega 500.
- is one of the five founders of Motor Racing Outreach.
- began the 1995 season with one team, by year's end was a part-owner of another.

In 1996, Bobby drove his white, red, and blue Jasper Motorsports Thunderbird with the same verve and power as always. And while the team's dedication has yet to provide the *consistent big paydays, success is only a single checkered flag away.*

When I was about ten, my father, Bobby Hillin, Sr., got interested in racing. I started going to the races with him on the weekends. I fell in love with the sport and decided right then that I wanted to be a race car driver. From that day forward, everything I did was geared toward that.

All throughout growing up and my teenage years, I spent a lot of time with my father while my mother and my sisters stayed home. Our attitude was, if we didn't do anything that would get us thrown in jail, then we were pretty good people. I had no knowledge whatsoever of the Bible, God, Satan, or Jesus Christ. All I knew was that I was a good person. My number-one goal in life was to please my father. He and I were very close, and we're still close today. Through it all he's seen me take some pretty hard knocks.

When I was five years old, I was diagnosed with typhoid fever, but they didn't know what it was until I'd been in the hospital for ten days and had come close to death. They figured it out and caught it at the last minute.

Then, when I was eight, I was run over by a station wagon. The front and rear wheels went over me. The doctors said it was a miracle that I survived. I still have the scars on my body and head from it, all these years later.

And when I was eleven, I had a bad pain in the back of my leg and no one knew what it was. For a year, I couldn't sleep through the night. Finally, a doctor diagnosed a tumor in the bone. The doctor had to strip away the calf muscle and saw the leg in two to get to it. But the doctor opened up the wrong leg! He cut through the muscle to the bone before he figured it out. Then he had to sew it back up. Today I have matching scars on both legs, from knee to ankle. Fortunately, he was able to get all of the cancer in the *other* leg and the bone fused back together.

Even through my wild days of high school, I knew God had a plan for me, even though I didn't know anything about Him. I knew that there was something special ahead for me. My parents, who never took me to church, even told me, "God's got something in store for you after all you've survived."

But because of my father's preoccupation with racing, my mom and dad grew apart. They had more problems, and the home was finally broken up. My father left when I was fourteen. I went with him, and my sisters stayed with my mother. All I had was racing.

At one point, about the ninth grade, I went to an organization called Young Life. Young Life explained the Bible, the Old Testament, and the New Testament to me. It explained that in the Old Testament, Satan tempted Adam and Eve to sin and therefore we're all descendants of sinners, born with a sinful nature.

For the first time, I learned what sin was, that sin was anything I did, said, or thought that is not pleasing to God. I learned that sin is a lot more than something that could get you thrown in jail. I also learned that no matter how hard I tried, I couldn't live a perfect life. I saw that even all of those great people in the Old Testament kept sinning and having to make sacrifices to God.

I also saw all of the references in the Old Testament where God kept telling His people that He was going to send a Savior and if we believe in His Savior, we will be forgiven of our sins. God said this Savior would give us an example of how to live a life that would be pleasing to God. And through this Savior, we would be saved from our sins.

Then, in the New Testament, I learned for the very first time how Jesus Christ came to earth as God's Son and *did* live a sinless life for us. I heard how this perfect Jesus died on a cross for all of us. For me. If we give our hearts to this Jesus, and we believe in Him, I learned that we will be forgiven of all our sins and we'll be made right with God. Finally, I heard how God would give us His Holy Spirit so that we could have power over sin and live a life that's pleasing to Him.

That was the first point in my life that I started having a conviction about my own lifestyle and things that I did. But it was only head knowledge then.

From there I moved to North Carolina to start racing. I started attending the chapel services at the races, but that was mainly because I thought that was the thing to do. I thought, *Maybe if I go to these chapel services, God will smile on me and let me win a race!*

I happened to live at the Charlotte Motor Speedway down the

hall from another driver, Lake Speed, and his wife, Rice. Lake and Rice always invited me over for dinner and were real nice to me. They probably knew that I'd been out at the bars all night the night before. But they never judged me; they accepted me for who I was. They were my friends. And slowly, gently, they taught the Bible to me. Through my friendship with them, I kept getting a stronger and stronger conviction in my own life. I just knew, deep down inside, that God wanted me to accept Jesus Christ as my personal Savior, just as Lake and Rice had done earlier.

This went on until one day there was a Bible study after the Friday practice at a racetrack, and they asked me to come. I said, "Maybe, but I want to go out to dinner with my crew."

After dinner, and when I returned that night, it just so happened that as I walking to my hotel room I had to walk right by the room where they were having the Bible study! The door was open, the curtains were open, the windows were up—everything. And from inside, they said, "Bobby! Bobby! Come on in!"

My heart began pounding. I went in and at the end of that evening, I prayed and received Jesus Christ into my heart.

I can honestly remember the weight being lifted off of my shoulders from my whole lifestyle because even at that age—nineteen or twenty—I was still carrying the burden of killing a cat when I was five years old. That's the kind of stuff I knew I was finally forgiven for. I was forgiven for the way I'd treated girls in high school, how I'd behaved—for everything! This feeling of forgiveness was a great thing.

I was so fortunate to have friends like Lake and Rice because they were so firm in their faith that they discipled me properly. They explained to me my need to make a public profession of faith.

I went the following Sunday, which was an off-week, to their church in Concord, North Carolina, and professed Christ publicly. That was a big step for me to say, "Hey, I'm telling everybody because I'm going to change my life. And I'm not going to change because of me, but because of Christ in me."

That's how it all came about.

One of the first things I did was to pray, "Lord, please help me quit cussing! Please give me the strength to quit." My mouth was filthy. It was the worst of the worst. Before, I'd tried on my own to quit; I couldn't do it. I'd embarrass myself in front of people it wasn't cool to cuss in front of.

And man! It was as if God turned the faucet off when I prayed that prayer! The bad words just quit coming out of my mouth. It was a miracle. That proved to me once again that God was alive inside my heart—this was real!

Meanwhile, a girl named Kim and I had dated in high school, but she was going to the University of Texas at the time and I was in North Carolina and we'd broken up. After my cussing prayer, I thought, *Who am I going to tell about this?* I was still a little nervous about telling my dad, so I called my ex-girlfriend. I said, "You're not going to believe what I did today."

Kim said, "What?"

I said, "I accepted Jesus Christ into my heart."

She said, "You're kidding me. You know, I did that as a young girl, but I fell away in high school. But since I've been in college, I've been involved in Bible studies, and I've rededicated my life to Christ!"

Kim had a Campus Crusade for Christ book titled *Ten Steps to Christian Maturity*. So I got one and we did the lessons together each night over the phone between Texas and North Carolina. And that's how we got back together. I asked Kim to marry me a year later.

Through all of this, I told my dad what happened. He didn't understand. He and his new girlfriend had been living together for several years. But not too much longer after I accepted Christ, his girlfriend did as well! All of a sudden, she got convicted and moved out, saying, "We're not going to live in sin here."

After losing her and thinking he'd lost me because I'd changed so much, my father locked himself up in his room and read the Bible for about a month! After that, *he* accepted Christ. And now they're married and have two children. God gave my father a second chance. We praise the Lord for that.

God's done amazing things in my life. My career's up and down, up and down. But every time I think it is over, God brings it back. What I always tell people today is this: "My number-one goal in life is still the same—to please my Father. But it is to please my heavenly Father."

Memorable Moment

It would have to be the day I won Talladega in 1986, my only win to date. That win made me the youngest driver to win a NASCAR race. It was a great year for me altogether. We had a really good superspeedway program—Daytona and Talladega were considered the big superspeedways back then. We'd finished fourth at the Daytona 500 and the year before at Talladega, we'd finished fourth. And on the Fourth of July race at Daytona we'd finished third. So we knew we were cookin'!

Going into that race, everything was great. We qualified thirteenth, then we went out and practiced on Saturday and we were real fast. We all went home that night thinking, *Hey! We are a contender for this race!*

And everything fell into place. There were a few rough moments. One in particular I remember was almost losing the car, trying to pass Dale Earnhardt—I had to back up and gather myself up and say, *Just settle down, you've got a fast car—take your time.* Another time my windshield got completely soaked with oil, and I was looking down out of my window at the white line as I drove around the racetrack at two hundred miles per hour. I needed to pull in but I didn't want to!

It was a great day, but I'm more determined now than ever to go on and win some more races.

DON HAWK

President/Business Manager, Dale Earnhardt, Inc.
#3
Richard Childress Racing
GM Goodwrench Service Chevrolet Monte Carlo

Don Hawk has always had racing in his blood. When he was a small boy, his family began going out to the local racetrack on Saturday nights. Later, he even owned a race car and did a little racing himself.

One Saturday night, Don and his race car made an intimate acquaintance with a wall. That night, his father suggested it might be wiser for Don to own cars in the future—and let someone else drive them.

Fast-forward a couple of decades, and young Don Hawk has been the business manager for two of the most successful drivers in NASCAR history, Dale Earnhardt and the late Alan Kulwicki. It certainly pays to listen to your father!

I came from a very church-oriented family, but I didn't come to faith in Christ until I was a junior in high school. We attended church as a ritual since we thought it was the right thing to do.

In 1971, before my junior year in high school, there was a speaker from the Moody Bible Institute with a week-long revival at a Bible camp with an old-fashioned tabernacle. The place seated about a thousand people. It was the July Fourth weekend, and a bunch of guys from the football team got invited by another guy who was a Christian, and *they* invited a bunch of cheerleaders to go. Finally we just decided after afternoon practice that we would go and find out what it was all about.

A couple of people went forward that night to accept Christ as their Savior. I wasn't quite sure about that. But for some reason—and I now understand that it was divine Providence—I went back on the Fourth of July, the last night of this rally. Once there, with some friends of mine, I listened and heard a very convicting message. I made a decision to go forward to accept Christ as my Savior, to come to faith in Him. I didn't understand what all I was committing myself to, but I knew I needed more than I had.

The amazing thing about it is, unbeknownst to me, attending the same service that night were my mother, father, and middle sister. When I looked to my right, about fifty yards away in this massive old tabernacle, kneeling at the altar, crying their tears, there they were! They had no clue I was there, I had no clue they were there. By the end of the evening, we were *all* kneeling on the same altar together, arms around each other, just crying.

Up until then, the high school had me under regular counseling. I spent a lot of time in the principal's office. My grades were terrible. They couldn't understand it because my achievement tests and IQ tests were showing that I was supposed to be doing a whole lot better than I was! In their words, I was "nonattentive." My parents came in quite a few times.

But when I came to faith before my junior year, I was on the honor roll six of the eight semesters that followed. I'm not saying this to brag, but to tell you how big the change was in my life. We formed our own Bible study in the chemistry lab, meeting at a quarter of seven in the morning. The chemistry teacher was a believer.

When I graduated from high school, the guidance counselors even asked me to come back to talk to the student body about the radical change in my life! (Back then you could talk about it in school.) I wouldn't classify myself as a Woodstock-type, pot-smoking drug addict, but I sure hadn't been doing the right things. If the analogy is racing, I was in the wrong line in the draft! The line I was supposed to be in was traveling on the outside at a good speed and I would every once in a while drift to the bottom and get alone—and that wasn't good.

One of the first things I did after I accepted Christ as my Savior was latch onto a book called *Mere Christianity* by C. S. Lewis. Ever since I came to faith, I've read that book at least once a year.

After high school, I went to college at Philadelphia College of the Bible. When I graduated from there in December of 1977, I decided I was going to go to Dallas Seminary.

All of a sudden, I made a U-turn in my career and said, "No, I'm not going to do that. I'm going back to the car business!" I went back to do what I did best—I knew cars and I tried to live a quality of life that was above reproach.

When I negotiated a deal, I tried to deal honestly, openly, with integrity, and I knew that if I did that in the business of servicing customers' cars or selling cars, they'd come back again because they knew they'd been treated right.

That's no different in this sport or any other business. If you treat people as they like to be treated, they will come back. It goes back to basic biblical principles. If you compromise your integrity, your credibility, your ethics, your morals, you're going to lose it all—whether you're a NASCAR Winston Cup driver, an accountant, a doctor, or a housewife. Once you compromise any of those, you're done.

This NASCAR thing started when I got a phone call from a guy representing Joe Gibbs, saying that Joe was going to start a race team, and he was looking for a Christian businessman who knew the automotive field. I'd worked eighteen years in the automotive field! He asked me if I'd be interested in being the general manager of their racing operation. And that whetted my appetite for racing. Later I went to work for Alan Kulwicki.

I've hit some speed bumps along the way. (My life centers around racing from a business perspective, so all of my analogies draw back to that.) The Christian life is not an oval. The Christian life is a road course. It's hills, it's right-hand turns, it's left-hand turns, it's long straightaways, it's short straightaways. All of that applies to the Christian life. And if you take it and look at it, if all we did was keep going in circles, it would be easy—anybody could do it. But you have to have the ability to sometimes turn left—and quickly turn right. You have to have the ability to brake and go down the hill and all of a sudden accelerate and go up the hill.

The times when I have to react and make changes in my life and confess my sins—and He is faithful and just to forgive my sins—are the times when I was supposed to make a hard left and I veered off a little to the right. You've got to be paying attention over every hill, every bump, around every curve, because you don't know where the course is going to lead you next. But you know it is going to lead you to a checkered flag when you get to the end.

Memorable Moment

I've had the real unfortunate experience of being a personal friend of Alan Kulwicki and going through Alan's death in a plane crash on April 1, 1993. At the same time, I've had the fortunate experience of being one of his best business colleagues and confidants. When Alan passed away, I was asked then to—and do to this day—represent Alan's estate. If somebody wants to do anything like a memorial or a souvenir, they either have to deal with the attorney, his father, or me.

Here's a guy who wins the 1992 Winston Cup Championship, and he only gets to celebrate it for three months. It was his lifelong dream. But Alan's favorite quote was, "It is far more important to *become* than to *acquire*." It's a philosophy that I've adopted since then. Alan used to say to me, "Hawk, if my goal is to become a millionaire, I'll never ever make it. If I want to acquire a million bucks, I'm not going to make it unless I become a Winston Cup champion. If I get the two confused, if I want to become a millionaire, I'm not going to acquire a championship. But if I acquire a championship, I probably will become a millionaire. You never can get those two confused."

About three months before Alan won his championship, a born-again Catholic priest led Alan to Christ.

I was part of Alan's memorial service in Charlotte. The good side is that the Lord turned that situation completely around, and I was personally offered a job by Dale Earnhardt. His exact words were, "I saw what you did and how you handled the Kulwicki estate and the team. I like what I see. I'd like you to spend some time with my wife and me; let us interview you. And I'd like for you to come to work for us."

I turned right around and Dale won the championship in '93, won it again in '94, and finished second in '95, and fourth in '96. Through it all, I'm pinching myself and saying, *I've seen the best of times and I've seen the worst of times. But I wouldn't trade it for anything.*

It has been a unique experience in that I've seen the valleys in the sport—when we lost a NASCAR Winston Cup champion—and then the Lord turns around and gives me a job with the guy who, on top of winning two in a row, his sixth and seventh championships, is tied with Richard Petty for the all-time lead.

That's what brought me from point A to point Z. I can only tell you that it's the hand of the Lord that took me here. I now know why—it's because I was to be with Alan, minister to Alan, share my faith with Alan, see Alan pass away, and be a part of Alan's ongoing legacy and estate. Then to hook up with another NASCAR Winston Cup champion and be a part of his life. It's been a unique experience!

APPENDIX 1
WHAT THE FLAGS MEAN

Green: Start of the race or the end of a danger previously signaled. The track is now clear.

Blue: Motionless—another competitor is following you and may be trying to pass. Waved—make way for another competitor who is trying to pass you.

Yellow: Motionless—danger, no passing, slow down. Waved—extreme danger, no passing, slow down, be prepared to stop.

White: One lap to go.

Yellow with vertical red stripes: Slippery surface, debris on the course.

Black: Furled—warning, you have committed a dangerous or unsportsmanlike move. Stop or you'll be penalized. Waved—stop in the pits for a consultation (usually displayed with the number of the car that broke the rule or displayed poor sportsmanship).

Black (shown to all): Interruption of practice or qualifying session because of a temporary difficulty. Take one cool-down lap and stop in the pits.

Black with orange disk: Your car has a mechanical problem you may or may not be aware of. Stop in the pits.

Red: The race is stopped. When this flag is displayed by the race director, drivers must slow down, cannot pass, and must proceed in single file to the pits.

Black-and-white-checkered flag: End of a session or race. Take one cool-down lap at slow speed and stop in the pits. (Unless you're the winner, of course, then you proceed to Victory Lane!)

1996 NASCAR WINSTON CUP SERIES

Feb. 11 Busch Clash of '96, Daytona Beach, FL
Winner: Dale Jarrett

Feb. 18 Daytona 500, Daytona Beach, FL Winner: Dale Jarrett

Feb. 25 Goodwrench 400, Rockingham, NC
Winner: Dale Earnhardt

Mar. 3 Pontiac Excitement 400, Richmond, VA
Winner: Jeff Gordon

Mar. 10 Purolator 500, Atlanta, GA Winner: Dale Earnhardt

Mar. 24 TransSouth Financial 400, Darlington, SC
Winner: Jeff Gordon

Mar. 31 Food City 500, Bristol, TN Winner: Jeff Gordon

Apr. 14 First Union 400, N. Wilkesboro, NC
Winner: Terry Labonte

Apr. 21 Goody's Headache Powders 500, Martinsville, NC
Winner: Rusty Wallace

Apr. 28 The Winston Select 500, Talladega, AL
Winner: Sterling Marlin

May 5 Save Mart Supermarkets 300, Sonoma, CA
Winner: Rusty Wallace

May 18 The Winston Select, Charlotte, NC
Winner: Michael Waltrip

May 26 Coca-Cola 600, Charlotte, NC Winner: Dale Jarrett

June 2 Miller 500, Dover, DE Winner: Jeff Gordon

June 16 UAW-GM Teamwork 500, Pocono, PA
Winner: Jeff Gordon

June 23 Miller 400, Brooklyn, MI Winner: Bobby Hamilton

July 6 Pepsi 40, Daytona Beach, FL Winner: Sterling Marlin

July 14 New Hampshire 300, Loudon, NH Winner:
Ernie Irvan

July 21 Miller 500, Pocono, PA Winner: Rusty Wallace

July 28 Diehard 500, Indianapolis, IN Winner: Jeff Gordon

Aug. 3 Brickyard 400, Indianapolis, IN Winner: Dale Jarrett

Aug. 11   The Bud at the Glen, Watkins Glen, NY
          Winner: Geoff Bodine
Aug. 18   GM Goodwrench Dealer 400, Brooklyn, MI
          Winner: Dale Jarrett
Aug. 24   Goody's Headache Powders 500, Bristol, TN
          Winner: Rusty Wallace
Sep. 1   Mountain Dew Southern 500, Darlington, SC
          Winner: Jeff Gordon
Sep. 7   Miller 400, Richmond, VA Winner: Ernie Irvan
Sep. 15   MBNA 500, Dover, DE Winner: Jeff Gordon
Sep. 22   Hanes 500, Martinsville, VA Winner: Jeff Gordon
Sep. 29   Tyson Holly Farms 400, N. Wilkesboro, NC
          Winner: Jeff Gordon
Oct. 6   UAW-GM Quality 500, Charlotte, NC
          Winner: Terry Labonte
Oct. 20   AC-Delco 400, Rockingham, NC Winner: Ricky Rudd
Oct. 27   Phoenix 500, Phoenix, AZ Winner: Bobby Hamilton
Nov. 10   Napa 500, Atlanta, GA Winner: Bobby Labonte

1996 NASCAR WINSTON CUP SERIES FINAL STANDINGS

Driver Position	Points	Winnings	Wins
1. Terry Labonte	4657	$1,939,213	2
2. Jeff Gordon	4620	$2,484,518	10
3. Dale Jarrett	4568	$2,343,750	4
4. Dale Earnhardt	4327	$1,725,396	2
5. Mark Martin	4278	$1,552,555	0
6. Ricky Rudd	3845	$1,213,373	1
7. Rusty Wallace	3717	$1,296,912	5
8. Sterling Marlin	3682	$1,315,050	2
9. Bobby Hamilton	3639	$952,625	1
10. Ernie Irvan	3632	$1,480,167	2
11. Bobby Labonte	3590	$1,362,415	1
12. Ken Schrader	3540	$979,287	0
13. Jeff Burton	3538	$729,852	0
14. Michael Waltrip	3535	$1,063,825	0
15. Jimmy Spencer	3476	$937,255	0
16. Ted Musgrave	3476	$868,555	0
17. Geoff Bodine	3218	$937,970	1
18. Rick Mast	3190	$835,532	0
19. Morgan Shepherd	3133	$638,597	0
20. Ricky Craven	3078	$865,362	0
21. Johnny Benson	3004	$893,580	0
22. Hut Stricklin	2854	$601,555	0
23. Lake Speed	2834	$789,175	0
24. Brett Bodine	2814	$741,716	0
25. Wally Dallenbach	2786	$794,501	0
26. Jeremy Mayfield	2721	$592,853	0
27. Kyle Petty	2696	$689,041	0
28. Kenny Wallace	2694	$457,665	0
29. Darrell Waltrip	2657	$740,185	0
30. Bill Elliott	2627	$706,506	0

Driver Position	Points	Winnings	Wins
31. John Andretti	2621	$688,511	0
32. Robert Pressley	2485	$690,465	0
33. Ward Burton	2411	$873,619	0
34. Joe Nemechek	2391	$666,247	0
35. Derrike Cope	2374	$675,781	0
36. Dick Trickle	2131	$404,927	0
37. Bobbly Hillin	2128	$382,724	0
38. Dave Marcis	2047	$435,177	0
39. Steve Grissom	1188	$314,983	0
40. Todd Bodine	991	$198,525	0

1996 NASCAR Busch Series
Grand National Division

Feb. 17   Daytona, FL   Goody's 300
           Winner: Steve Grissom

Feb. 24   Rockingham, NC   Goodwrench 200
           Winner: Mark Martin

Mar. 2   Richmond, VA   Hardee's Challenge 250
           Winner: Jeff Purvis

Mar. 9   Atlanta, GA   Busch Lite 300
           Winner: Terry Labonte

Mar. 17   Nashville, TN   Opryland USA 320
           Winner: Bobby Labonte

Mar. 23   Darlington, SC   Dura-Lube 200
           Winner: Mark Martin

Mar. 30   Bristol, TN   Goody's 250
           Winner: Mark Martin

Apr. 6   Hickory, NC   SunDrop 400
           Winner: David Green

May 19   Nazareth, PA   Meridian Advantage 200
           Winner: Randy Lajoie

May 25   Charlotte, NC   Red Dog 300
           Winner: Mark Martin

June 1   Dover, DL   GM/Goodwrench/Delco 200
           Winner: Randy Lajoie

June 8   South Boston, VA Winston Motorsports 300
           Winner: Todd Bodine

June 22   Myrtle Beach, SC Carolina Pride/Red Dog 250
           Winner: David Green

June 30   Watkins Glen, NY Lysol 200
           Winner: Terry Labonte

July 7	Milwaukee, WI	Sears Auto Center 250
	Winner: Buckshot Jones	
July 12	Loudon, NH	Stanley 200
	Winner: Randy Lajoie	
July 27	Talladega, AL	HumminBird 500K
	Winner: Greg Sacks	
Aug. 2	Indianapolis, IN	Kroger 200
	Winner: Randy Lajoie	
Aug. 17	Brooklyn, MI	Detroit Gasket 200
	Winner: Jeff Purvis	
Aug. 23	Bristol, TN	Food City 250
	Winner: Jeff Purvis	
Aug. 31	Darlington, SC	Dura-Lube 200
	Winner: Terry Labonte	
Sept. 6	Richmond, VA	AutoLite Platinum 250
	Winner: Kenny Wallace	
Sept. 14	Dover, DE	MBNA 200
	Winner: Randy Lajoie	
Oct. 5	Charlotte, NC	Bumper to Bumper 300
	Winner: Mark Martin	
Nov. 3	Homestead, FL	Jiffy Lube 300
	Winner: Kevin Lepage	

Appendix 5
Indy Racing League

1996

Indy 200 at Walt Disney World, February 1, 1996, Orlando, FL.
  Winner: Buzz Calkins
Dura-Lube 200, April 9, 1996, Phoenix, AZ.
  Winner: Arie Luyendyk
Indianapolis 500, May 28, 1996, Indianapolis, IN.
  Winner: Buddy Lazier
True Value 200, August 18, 1996, Loudon, NH.
  Winner: Scott Sharp
Las Vegas 200, September 15, 1996, Las Vegas, NV.
  Winner: Richie Hearn

1997

Indy 200 at Walt Disney World, January 25, 1997, Orlando, FL.
  Winner: Eddie Cheever
Phoenix 200 at PIR, March 23, 1997, Phoenix, AZ.
  Winner:
Indianapolis 500, May 25, 1997, Indianapolis, IN.
  Winner:
IRL Longhorn 500 at the Texas Motor Speedway, June 7, 1997,
  Dallas, TX.
  Winner:

1996 NASCAR BUSCH SERIES GRAND NATIONAL DIVISION FINAL STANDINGS

 1. Randy LaJoie   3714
 2. David Green   3685
 3. Todd Bodine   3064
 4. Jeff Green   3059
 5. Chad Little   2984
 6. Jason Keller   2900
 7. Jeff Purvis   2894
 8. Kevin Lepage   2870
 9. Phil Parsons   2854
10. Mike KcLaughlin   2853

1996 PPG INDY CAR WORLD SERIES

Mar. 3   Grand Prix of Miami Metro-Dade
Homestead Motorsports Complex
Winner: Jimmy Vasser

Mar. 17   Rio 400 Nelson Piquet International Raceway
Winner: Andre Ribeiro

Mar. 31   IndyCar Australia Surfers Paradise,
Queensland, Australia
Winner: Jimmy Vasser

Apr. 14   Toyota Grand Prix of Long Beach Long Beach, CA
Winner: Jimmy Vasser

Apr. 28   Bosch Spark Plug Grand Prix Nazareth Speedway
Winner: Michael Andretti

May 26   U.S. 500 Michigan International Speedway
Winner: Jimmy Vasser

June 2   Miller 200 The Milwaukee Mile
Winner: Michael Andretti

June 9   ITT Automotive Detroit Grand Prix
The Raceway at Belle Island
Winner: Michael Andretti

June 23   Budweiser/G.I. Joe 200
Portland International Raceway
Winner: Alex Zanardi

June 30   Medic Drug Grand Prix of Cleveland
Cleveland, OH
Winner: Gil De Ferran

July 14   Molson Indy Toronto Toronto, Ontario, Canada
Winner: Adrian Fernandez

July 28   Michigan 500 Michigan International Speedway
Winner: Andre Ribeiro

Aug. 11   Miller 200 Mid-Ohio Sports Car Course
Winner: Alex Zanardi

Aug. 18   Texaco/Havoline 200 Road America
Winner: Michael Andretti

Sept. 1   Molson Indy Vancouver Vancouver, B.C., Canada
Winner: Michael Andretti

Sept. 8   Toyota Grand Prix of Monterey/Bank of
America 300 Laguna Seca Raceway, Monterey, CA
Winner: Alex Zanardi

APPENDIX 8
1996 PPG INDY CAR
WORLD SERIES FINAL STANDINGS

Rank	Points	Name
1.	154	Jimmy Vasser
2.	132	Michael Andretti
(tie)		
2.	132	Alex Zanardi
4.	125	Al Unser, Jr.
5.	110	Christian Fittipaldi
6.	104	Gil de Ferran
7.	102	Bobby Rahal
8.	87	Bryan Herta
(tie)		
8.	87	Greg Moore
10.	82	Scott Pruett
11.	76	Andre Riberiro
12.	71	Adrian Fernandez
13.	60	Paul Tracy
14.	53	Mauricio Gugelmin
15.	43	Stefan Johansson
16.	41	Mark Blundell
17.	33	Parker Johnstone
18.	29	Robbie Gordon
(tie)		
18.	29	Emerson Fittipaldi
20.	26	Eddie Lawson

ABOUT THE AUTHORS

Robert Darden is the author of twenty-five books including *The Way of an Eagle* with P .J. Richardson (Thomas Nelson), *Too Close to My Heart* with Mary Darden and Susan Tevis (Kensington), *I, Jesus* (Summit), and *Mad Man in Waco* with Brad Briley (WRS). He is the editor of the religious humor and satire magazine *The Door*, and teaches professional writing and screenplay writing at Baylor University. Robert and his wife, Mary, live in Waco with their three children. He is a deacon at Seventh and James Baptist church.

P. J. Richardson is president and chief executive officer of Reeves Manufacturing Inc., an emergency medical, firefighter and safety equipment manufacturer. He is the coauthor of *The Way of an Eagle* (with Bob Darden). He is active in the Fellowship of Christian Athletes and is well known in golfing and motor-racing circles. He and his wife, Billie, live in Frederick, Maryland, and have two children.